THE DEATH OF THE CRITIC

The Death of the Critic

Rónán McDonald

continuum

Continuum
The Tower Building
11 York Road
London SE1 7NX

80 Maiden Lane, Suite 704
New York
NY 10038

www.continuumbooks.com

British Library Cataloguing-in-Publication Data
A catalogue record for this book is available from the British Library.

ISBN 978 08264 9279 1 (hardback)

ISBN 978 08264 9280 7 (paperback)

Typeset by Data Standards Ltd, Frome, Somerset

Contents

For Sarah

Preface

This short book is a sympathetic treatment of the fortunes of criticism and an argument for its cultural importance. When I told people that I was writing a book called 'The Death of the Critic' they immediately assumed I was writing a celebration, not a eulogy. 'Good for you!' was often the response. 'Make sure you put the boot in for me.' It is no surprise that some acquaintances thought I was grave-dancing. The critic has long enjoyed a low reputation. He (and traditionally the critic was male and patrician) has often been regarded as a parasite, strangely ineffectual in his inability to create art himself but inappropriately powerful in his capacity to ruin reputations with the stroke of a poison pen. What is there to mourn if this elitist figure from a more authoritarian era is now disappearing? Surely it is to be welcomed that the public feel able to make their own choices about what they watch or read, without genuflecting to the so-called 'expert'? Can the proliferation of blogs and discussion groups be signs of popular empowerment, whereby consumers of the arts make their own choices and share their own enthusiasms with their peers? We are told that 'people power' is now the dominant force.

The age of the critic as the arbiter for public taste and cultural consumption seems to have passed. It does seem that the status of the critic across the arts is much lower now than it was in the 1950s or 1960s. There are still gifted and informed drama, art and film critics, many of them writing in newspapers and magazines, others based in universities producing valuable academic work. There are multitudinous venues for criticism across the print media and in the virtual world. But the role has diminished since the heyday of Kenneth Tynan, Clement Greenberg or Pauline Kael. Perhaps the critic has died because, as Old Father Time says in *Jude the Obscure*, 'we are too menny'. When there are so many critical voices raised, it is not surprising that few are heard above the din.

Unavoidably, the critic occupies a hierarchical role: someone who knows more about an artform than we do, whose opinion or interpretation is worthy of special regard. This hierarchical aspect has fallen victim to the wider shifts in social relations, away from deference and authority. Evaluation of the arts has been dispersed, beauty emphatically ascribed to the 'eye of the beholder', not the expert critic or the aesthetician.

There is no one cause for the death of the critic. But the issue with which this book is particularly concerned, shifting attitudes towards value and evaluation, draws in many others. Is artistic quality simply a question of personal likes and dislikes? Is one opinion as good as another? Or is there any way that quality or value judgements about art can be grounded in any objective or external criteria? These are very old and very difficult questions. But they have been pushed aside in academic circles in recent years. High-profile critics of the mid-twentieth century were frequently university professors who wrote books and reviews for a non-academic audience. Such figures are less culturally dominant now.

Chapter One puts forward the general case for the 'death of the critic' in contemporary culture, attending to attitudes towards artistic values and evaluation. It concludes with a rejoinder to John Carey's recent, relativist polemic *What Good Are The Arts?* (2005). Chapter Two is a necessarily selective history of criticism, assessing the various cleavages between critical values and the wider cultural attitudes to art and literature. Chapter Three looks at the development of literary criticism within and outside the university during the twentieth century. Academic criticism often felt the need to firm up its disciplinary foundations, an impulse that led it to seek various rapprochements with scientific methodology. But this generated contradictions with the non-scientific role of literature, including that which justified its presence on the syllabus in the first place. Chapter Four suggests that the arrival of 'theory' in the late 1960s, despite its revolutionary, iconoclastic fervour, involves crucial continuities with the previous generation of criticism. It assesses the impact of structuralism, post-structuralism and cultural studies and concludes with detecting signs of a 'new aestheticism' at the vanguard of literary theory.

This contraction of academic criticism and the dilation of reviewing are not opposite trends but covertly part of the same ethos. They both involve a renunciation of the idea that the value of art and literature can be discussed or argued about with any authority. The cleft public sphere once occupied by the critic comes from the presumption that evaluative criticism is a question, simply, of personal taste. This book tries to make an alternative case. That much-maligned figure – the Critic – has played an important role in the history of art and culture. His death should not be celebrated.

Healthy public criticism has often involved close connections between the academic study of the arts and wider reviewing culture. Though academics still write for newspapers, the intellectual connections have significantly diminished. Even if one person undertakes both roles, reviewers and university professors are engaged in significantly different tasks. Common ground between the academic monograph and the interests of a wide audience has become ever more attenuated.

The key factor in separating academic from non-academic criticism, I argue, is the turn from evaluative and aesthetic concerns in the university humanities' departments. The issue of the 'canon', of what is worthy of study and why, was paramount in earlier generations. For better or worse, Matthew Arnold's counsel that we should 'endeavour to learn and to propagate the "best" that is known and taught in the world' was an implicit touchstone until the end of 1960s. However, the rise of cultural studies led to a radical change of emphasis: a general suspicion not just of canon formation but of aesthetic judgement as a whole. The neo-Marxist orientation of cultural studies regards the 'best' as a politically dubious category, with selections made in its name often nurturing hidden and hierarchical agendas.

So the public critic has been dismembered by two opposing forces: the tendency of academic criticism to become increasingly inward-looking and non-evaluative, and the momentum for journalistic and popular criticism to become a much more democratic, dispersive affair, no longer left in the hands of the experts. This book seeks to trace in particular the disconnection between the academic critic and a wider public audience, paying special attention to literary criticism. Its governing theme is the fate of evaluation and the basis on which it is built.

I would like to thank several individuals who have helped me during the writing of this book. Mark Bostridge was encouraging and helpful during the conception of the project while, at Continuum, Robin Baird-Smith, Andrew Walby, Sarah Patel amd Anya Wilson have been supportive, enthusiastic, efficient and patient. From the beginning Frances Wilson has been an outstanding advocate from the start and I would like to thank her for our many conversations about the project, for her invaluable help in finding the right publisher, and for her feedback and encouragement during its composition. Ray Ryan has, as ever, been an adamantine counseller, a generous goad, and a painstaking and perceptive reader to whom I owe much. Gerald Lang also kindly read the manuscript and helped clarify some philosophical points. Sarah Montgomery has read and re-read drafts of this manuscript, giving me excellent advice and suggestions throughout. She has been a balm against self-doubt, a prod to productivity and has inspired and enriched this book in ways too numerous to list. This book is dedicated to her.

CHAPTER ONE

The Value of Criticism

*I took it seriously. We all did. We hung around the place
talking about literary criticism. We sat in pubs and
coffee bars talking about W. K. Wimsatt and G. Wilson
Knight, about Richard Hoggart and Northrop Frye,
about Richard Poirier, Tony Tanner and George Steiner.*

(xi–xii)

I

Thus the novelist Martin Amis remembers the 'age of
criticism'. It ran, according to Amis, from about 1948, the
year of T. S. Eliot's *Notes Towards a Definition of Culture* and
F. R. Leavis's *The Great Tradition*, and tailed off in the social
and economic turmoil of the early 1970s. It was as if the
energies that fuelled the flourishing experimentalism in art
and literature after the First World War, known collectively as
'modernism', found a home in criticism after the Second.
Modernism, often notoriously difficult, needed its critics and
explicators to bring it to a perplexed audience, and many of
the great modernist writers, like Virginia Woolf and T. S. Eliot,
were themselves masterful critics and theorists. So it is not
surprising that modernism would, at least for a generation,
raise the tide upon which criticism floated.

It is striking, however, how quickly it subsided. There are few such conversations about the esteemed arbiters of taste today, no obvious names now to tutor the literary passions of the aspiring novelist. For better or worse, the baton has not been passed on to a few, anointed successors, but has rather been thrown to the many, to the book club and the Booker judge, the bloggers and the pundits. The public critic, who has the authority to shape public taste, with enough respect and penetration to direct public attention to new artists or movements, seems to have gone the way of the rag-and-bone man or the bus conductor, no longer a figure for which a late capitalist society has much use.

Explaining the change, Amis points a finger at the 'forces of democratization', for which the hierarchies and echelons of critical expertise were a ready target (xii). A key moment was surely the anti-authoritarianism of 1968, with its student riots and revolutionary fervour. An elite coterie of aging university dons, pronouncing upon what the rest of us should read, is not going to win a sympathetic ear at the barricades. This was also the year when Roland Barthes famously declared the 'death of the author'. Reading, Barthes maintains, is a fluid, open-ended, individualized process that does not need to heed the author's intentions to be legitimate. If you want to tackle authority, take on the author.

For Barthes our reverence for authorial intention is a relatively recent, post-Enlightenment phenomenon that we must move beyond. Any objection to a critical approach that says 'that's not what the author meant' illegitimately curtails language's fecundity and the potential plurality of meanings in a literary work. Barthes's essay – still *de rigueur* for university undergraduates – is a clarion call for freedom and liberation. It welcomes the 'death of the author' because it heralds the 'birth of the reader'.

Killing the author, and such associated concepts as 'creativity', 'imagination', 'design', and 'inspiration', may liberate the reader to revel in the pleasures of free interpretation. But it also seems to have done away with the critic. Or at least with the literary critic as public intellectual, a figure to whom a wide audience might look as a judge of quality or a guide to meaning.

There is no shortage of reviewing. Newspapers devote swathes of space to their arts coverage. Publications like the *Times Literary Supplement* and the *London Review of Books*, the *New York Review of Books* and the *New Yorker* fill a market for high-level niche journalism. But quantity is no substitute for authority. Critics with a large recognition factor outside academic circles are rare, especially if we exclude figures like Germaine Greer or the late Edward Said, known more for their political activism than their criticism. How many books of literary criticism have made a substantial public impression in the last 20 years? Literary biography thrived in the 1990s, despite Barthes's manifesto on its irrelevance. History, psychology, evolutionary biology and popular science colonize the non-fiction sections of the bookshops. But books of criticism seem comparatively absent. During the 1970s and 1980s, academic literary criticism receded almost wholly into the university campus, its outcome confined to specialized monographs and scholarly journals. Academics in other subjects with a gift for popularizing their subject, like Richard Dawkins and Stephen Hawking, Simon Schama and A. C. Grayling, command large non-academic audiences and enjoy high media profiles. However, there are very few literary critics who take on this role for English.

When it comes to literary criticism, the acreage in newspapers and magazines devoted to 'reviewing' is no substitute for the authority of hard covers.

From one point of view it might seem absurd to speak of the death of the critic when everybody now seems to be one. It takes an army of reviewers to fill the arts pages and Sunday supplements. And critical response is no longer confined to the printed word. Recent years have seen the explosion of the reading group, the book club and the internet blog. Amazon famously sports readers' reviews on its webpage and bookshops tag shelves with the favourite books of their staff. Everyone has an opinion and one opinion is 'as good as another'. Television programmes and newspapers are full of phone-ins and 'You Decide' polls, in which the media make a show of consulting the public and eliciting their views and opinions. Interactive media come swaddled in the rhetoric of popular enfranchisement. Cynics might sneer that these claims for 'people power' are a patronising parody of real democracy, but there is nonetheless a felt imperative to reach out and involve the consumer and citizen. If academic criticism, with its armoury of theoretical language, has 'retreated' into the universities, a reciprocal, centrifugal force has meant that We Are All Critics Now. Here at least, it seems, the promised birth of the reader has allowed a much wider articulation of artistic response.

The era of the experts, the informed cognoscenti whose judgements and tastes operated as a lodestar for the public, has seemingly been swept aside by a public that has laid claim to its capacity to evaluate its own cultural consumption. The contraction of academic criticism and the expansion of reviewing are both symptoms of the same anti-authoritarianism: a refusal of top-down instruction and a suspicion of hierarchy. The critic-as-instructor, as objective judge and expert, has yielded to the critic who shares personal reactions and subjective enthusiasms. If anyone can be a critic, then there is hardly any need for specialized and devoted professionals.

These tendencies have been accelerated in recent years by the arrival of the internet, which gives an easily accessible platform for readers to share every peeve and passion, bypassing even the remaining authority of the paid newspaper reviewer. The proliferation of literary blogs is a vivid example of the devolution of critical authority. Such accessible forums for discussion and debate have many beneficial aspects and, given the already wide variety and quality of these blogs, generalizations are unwise. You can find very bad writing and sloppy impressionism in literary blogs, but also incisive, fresh, thoughtful criticism from voices unencumbered by the politics of Grub Street. Dismayed voices have been raised against the lack of unaccountability of the bloggers; anonymity and the absence of editorial control allow them, allegedly, to defame, slander and abuse authors willy-nilly. But bloggers can defend against these complaints by pointing out that the sheer size and inclusivity of the blogosphere dilutes *ad hominem* attacks. And the positive effects of internet 'anonymity' means that the blogosphere escapes the favouritism, back-scratching and score-settling that often goes on in the newspapers and literary reviews. After all, the historian Richard Hofstadter once slyly remarked that the *New York Review of Books* might be more accurately entitled the *New York Review of Each Others' Books*.

Neither triumphalist declarations of 'people power' nor jeremiads about falling standards seem quite adequate at these early stages of the blogosphere. Yet already there are signs of a stand-off, of acrimony and polarization between the bloggers and the established literary journalists. Writing in the *Sunday Telegraph* on 12 November 2006, John Sutherland, Professor of English at University College London and a regular *Guardian* journalist, raised worries about the proliferation of blogging culture. His article was prompted by a vicious (and unaccountable) Amazon review, but he also made some general criticisms of the blogging phenomenon:

> There are those who see web-reviewing (whether independent bloggery or commercially hosted) as a 'power to the reader' trend – the democratization of something traditionally monopolized by literary mandarins. And there are those who see it as a degradation of literary taste.

The article, which tended towards the 'degradation of literary taste' position, unleashed a whirlwind. The novelist Susan Hill, a keen blogger, was amongst the more restrained – 'How dare one of these "literary mandarins" feel they are above us and by implication, above book buyers and readers? Who do they think they are to lord it over us?' It was as if the bloggers had issued their first *fatwa*. Interviewed on BBC Radio 4's *Today* programme as the controversy intensified, Sutherland claimed that he had received death threats. Each side sneered at the other. The bloggers pointed at the elitist irrelevance and superfluity of the newspaper reviewers in the new democratic dispensation; the journalists suggested that the blogosphere is peopled by obsessive cranks with too much time on their hands. As Rachel Cooke, an *Observer* journalist on the Sutherland side, remarked, 'this is an early scuffle in what will undoubtedly prove to be one of the great arguments of our time. Battle lines are being drawn.'

But the debate is much wider than the journalists versus the bloggers, the paid versus the unpaid. At its heart is the question of what constitutes the value of a book or a film or a work of art and, relatedly, who is qualified to gauge it. Does expertise and professional training make one critic's views more valid than another's? Does it even make sense to say that one literary work is 'better' than another, as if artistic quality were quantifiable and measurable? Is the value of the art intrinsic to the work or simply in the subjective response of the viewer? Does beauty ever get outside the eye of the beholder? These are hardly new questions, but participants in contemporary debate often take one position or another on them, overtly or not.

Defending the 'blogosphere' above the printed literary review, web writers often claim that they would rather get their recommendations from someone they know, someone with the same outlook and taste as them. The want to read or watch what they know they will enjoy, not what the expert deems worthy of attention. One obvious problem with this is that readers and viewers are relying on a reviewing system that confirms and assuages their prejudices and inclinations rather than challenging them. An able and experienced critic, with sufficient respect and authority, could traditionally persuade readers to give unfamiliar work a second chance, to see things they did not see at a first glance. Put simply, this is one of the reasons why a healthy public criticism provides such a salutary service for the arts: it can brush received wisdoms and tired forms against the grain. In that respect, trained critics, despite their fusty reputation, can be the harbingers of the new.

But the blogosphere, flushed with its growing power, often scorns the print review culture and the idea of the critic-as-expert. Told to know its place, it cries 'elitism' and 'intellectual superiority'. Hill concludes:

The fact is that the tide has turned and the people have power now ... the many – with honourable exceptions – arrogant, lazy, stuck-in-the-mud, cliquey little set of literary editors, and/ or 'mandarins' are now almost totally irrelevant. One day, their editors will wake up to the fact and give over their space to Curling, or Dominoes. One day.

While the circumstances here are new, the sentiments behind this grave-dancing are not. If the critic's judgement once held much greater sway than today, people have often regarded the job as inconsequential, secondary and even disreputable, falling short of an honest day's work. Common speech deploys the distinction of 'creative writing' to refer to fiction, poetry or drama (with a dispensation for non-fictional, but high-selling, genres like memoir or biography), implying that criticism is non-creative, derivative and merely secondary. The critic is seen as the parasite on the back of the artist. For all their presumptions of intellectual superiority and privileged judgement, critics are, at best, the subservient explicators of the 'creative' arts, at worst their resentful usurpers. They compensate for their own lack of talent and ingenuity by undermining those with the wherewithal and energy to go out and 'do it' themselves. Not many adolescents dream of becoming the next Sir Arthur Quilter-Couch.

In the UK in particular, the role is sometimes associated in the public mind with hoary and dated old class divisions, an association that is encapsulated and caricatured by the pursed lips and squashed, Edwardian vowels of the *Evening Standard* art critic Brian Sewell, whose public persona is so often mocked. Or else it evokes the insufferably pretentious strata of the middle classes, such as that parodied by *Viz* comic in its strip 'The Critics', where the smug, shark-faced couple, Natasha and Crispin Critic are shallow, sycophantic, elitist, snobbish and hypocritical people who live in a cliquish, privileged and smug social circle.

Little wonder, then, that when critics appear in public or in the media, their job designation often pops up decently clothed by another, more respectable role: 'writer and critic', 'journalist and critic', 'academic and critic' – anything but the bald 'critic' on its own. If the critic is not regarded as a dog-in-the-manger or a parasite, the role carries a whiff of the merely dilettantish or fey, not really a proper job in itself. Though many of the Romantic poets made enormous contributions to the history of criticism and aesthetics, little of the Romantic aura of creativity ever brushed off on the critic. It seems the creative imagination can illuminate the real world, but not the artistic work.

Nobody has more disdain for the critic than 'creative' artists themselves. Everything the public dislikes about the critics is exacerbated for them by professional fear and resentment. 'Don't pay any attention to what the critics say,' is Sibelius's oft-quoted advice, 'no statue has ever been erected over a critic.' It has been a consolation to many aspirant musicians and artists (notwithstanding the statue of the great French critic, Charles-Augstin Saint-Beuve, in the Luxembourg Gardens in Paris). The Irish playwright Brendan Behan puts the same notion more spikily: 'Critics are like eunuchs in a harem; they know how it is done, they've seen it done every day, but they're unable to do it themselves.'

Among all the arts, the theatre is probably the one where the critic – because so traditionally powerful – evokes the strongest loathing and contempt. Often the frustration is understandable. The history of drama criticism reveals many a blemished record, with reviewers frequently failing to under-stand or appreciate experiment or innovation. They have often pilloried or ridiculed plays that later achieve lasting importance. Perhaps the neatest slide of the rapier from any playwright comes from George Bernard Shaw, himself a critic and reviewer of considerable import, when he remarked: 'A drama critic is a man who leaves no turn unstoned.' Shaw clearly had in mind the unimaginative and staid reviewer, hostile to the inventive, seminal stagecraft. Yet, while the majority of timid and conformist reviewers perhaps merited the rebuke, there were others, surely, who played a key role in elaborating, appreciating and immortalizing the shock of the new in the theatre.

Take the case of Samuel Beckett, a playwright who once described literary criticism, with mordant vividness, as 'hysterectomies with a trowel'. He makes 'critic' the most grievous insult that can be hurled in his *Waiting for Godot*:

VLADIMIR: Moron!
ESTRAGON: Vermin!
VLADIMIR: Abortion!
ESTRAGON: Morpion!
VLADIMIR: Sewer rat!
ESTRAGON: Curate!
VLADIMIR: Cretin!
ESTRAGON [*With finality*]: Crritic!
VLADIMIR: Oh!
[*He wilts, vanquished, and turns away.*] (67)

Perhaps anticipating some of the scornful notices that his avant-garde play would initially receive, Beckett got his retaliation in first. An avant-garde play like *Waiting for Godot* alienates and frustrates some reviewers, as it did its early audiences.

But, ironically, it was precisely through the offices of the loathed critics, in the form of Kenneth Tynan and Harold Hobson, that *Waiting for Godot* came to be hailed as the most important play of the twentieth century. The favourable judgements of these respected Sunday broadsheet reviewers created the controversy, eclipsing the scornful notices that had already appeared in the London dailies. Beckett's reputation was created by theatre critics like these and subsequently, like so many of the modernists who preceded him, by high-profile academic critics, in his case Hugh Kenner, Ruby Cohn and Harold Bloom.

Today, would there be critics of similar status to mediate between a radical artistic work and resistant public taste? David Hare has argued that the quality of writing about the theatre has deteriorated: 'Since the days when Ronald Bryden "discovered" Tom Stoppard via *Rosencrantz and Guildenstern are Dead* on the Edinburgh fringe, there has not been a single critic whose name can be identified with a single writer in the way that Tynan championed Osborne and Harold Hobson supported Beckett.' But this may not be down to the deterioration of writing about the theatre per se, so much as a shift in the public's relationship with the critics.

Perhaps the question of 'resistant taste' is now a redundant one. The public's intolerance has worn thin. A *succès de scandale* or an intellectual hit like *Waiting for Godot* does not seem very likely now, in an age of Sarah Kane and the Chapman Brothers. Contemporary audiences are glutted on the unorthodox and shocking in the visual arts. Each year, tabloid newspapers in Britain line up to sneer at the Turner Prize, but that they expect to do so indicates just how orthodox the supposedly iconoclastic has now become. The 2006 Turner Prize really did raise eyebrows, because the award actually went to a painter. Perhaps the advanced capitalist era is too hedonistic and amnesiac for the avant-garde or innovative to have an impact. There is no platform, no social vehicle for critique. The strange and outlandish has been domesticated and absorbed, not least by a lucrative contemporary art market, where a major dealer has vastly more effect on the esteem in which an artwork is held than any critic.

It is not simply a wail of nostalgia for a romanticized 'public sphere' to point out that, in the past, vital artistic innovations and cultural movements have benefited from a healthy critical culture, one reliant on experts and specialists. At such times, art needs criticism. Would the world have taken to Turner without the offices of John Ruskin? Jackson Pollock without Clement Greenberg? The modernist movements of the late nineteenth and early twentieth century, in particular, were highly reliant on their interpreters. Without Arthur Symons's *The Symbolist Movement in Literature* (1899), which T. S. Eliot identified as having changed the course of his life, French symbolism would not have come to England to revolutionize the written word. Would the critics who introduced the often difficult, modernist literary works of the early twentieth century – Edmund Wilson, Richard Ellmann, R. P. Blackmur – have much impact in the current critical climate? If not, could we rely on the bloggers to bring the shock of the new to a wide audience? The conviction that educated taste is an elitist ruse, that one opinion is as good as another, and that we should take our lead for our cultural life solely from *people like us* might seem like a powerful instance of people power. But if we only listen to those who already share our proclivities and interests, will not the supposed critical democracy lead instead to a dangerous attenuation of taste and conservatism of judgement?

II

Before we celebrate the passing of the 'elitist' critic we should remember this historical relationship between new and vital art and the mechanisms of its critical reception and mediation. This might be one of the reasons why so many of the great modernist writers, like Yeats, Eliot, and Woolf, took their own critical writings so seriously. As I suggested earlier, the flourishing of criticism that occurred in the post-war period was a product of modernism in retreat. Faced with the challenge of *Ulysses* (1922), *The Waste Land* (1922) or Pound's *Cantos* (1930–69), a new critical idiom was needed that could provide a renovated mode of apprehension, appropriate to the thickened textures and opaque forms of these modernist monuments. It was found in rigorous close textual analysis and a strenuous engagement with verbal detail. These techniques of close-reading and attention to the text, outside the historical or philological concerns of traditional literary scholarship, came to be known as the 'New Criticism'. Its impetus may have been modernist but its methods and techniques were applied to literary texts from all periods.

In recent decades, literary theorists have repudiated New Critical procedures for an allegedly evasive aversion to history, its 'formalism' supposedly uprooted the works from the contexts in which they are set, treating the historical moment as if in quarantine from the words on the page. We have seen in recent decades divisive methodological differences in university humanities departments, riven by the 'theory wars' of the 1980s and 1990s. It might be remembered that in the 1950s and 1960s the New Critics were often looked down upon as amateurs by the old-style scholars and philologists, who walked the same corridors. Close-reading of poetry, however brilliant, did not seem quite so serious a business as doing 'proper' research in an archive. If in the 1980s the frosty stares were between theorists and traditionalists, the black polo necks against the tweed jackets, in the 1950s it was the critics against the scholars.

But the New Criticism had a huge influence outside the university. Its techniques of close attention to the words on the page involved a rigour that was an antidote to mere impressionism. Yet its methods were accessible and unspecialized enough to mould the teaching of English in secondary schools for decades. As we shall see in Chapter 3, placing literature itself at the centre of attention and emphasizing artistic value and the so-called 'canon' of great and enduring literature fired the importance of criticism within the public realm. Because literature was taken seriously, was presented as valuable in itself (not as an aperture into social and historical contexts); the criticism which sought to illuminate and interpret it was also valuable. This fed the post-war penetration of critical writing whereby a literate public read and discussed the writings of prominent critics. Criticism elevated literature, insisted in its various ways that culture mattered. In doing so, it also elevated itself.

The New Critics were closely associated with poetry, which leant itself to the methods of close-reading they advocated. Could it be that the notoriously tiny and shrinking market for poetry now is related to the atrophy in critical connections between the academy and the literate public? Poetry has, along with the criticism which accompanies it, retreated into the universities. Meanwhile poets supplement their meagre sales by taking on university affiliations. While populists and anti-modernists call for a 'return' to accessible verse and conventional rhyme, academic theorists demand that poetry and poetry criticism pays its dues to the university climate of ethnic diversity and postmodern theory. In the academy, poetry is subjected to esoteric and opaque theorization, while all too often literary journalism treats it tokenistically or impressionistically.

The circle is self-perpetuating: the more poetry seeks the endorsement of the universities, the more poetry criticism becomes absorbed by academic language and less a part of a common critical culture that might engage non-experts. Part of the problem, as Marjorie Perloff points out in a excellent essay on the treatment of poetry in magazines and news-papers, is the proclivity of contemporary literary supplements to commission round-up reviews of numerous, disparate volumes, more in a gesture towards the traditional prestige of poetry than an effort to engage with the contemporary scene. Perloff ends on an optimistic note, with the hope that the internet may provide a critical forum for discussion of challenging or innovative poetry, but this too has its problems and dangers, some touched on already. One is quality control. Internet reviewers are not always as accountable as their counterparts in the print media; fact-checking and accuracy are not as audited. This is not to cast a pall over the standards of the many reliable and professional internet magazines and reviews, that are proliferating and growing in profile and prestige all the time. But ease of access, for all its benefits, can imperil reliability.

There is another, less obvious, danger. The internet provides space for criticism and analysis of niche interests, which, because of space limitations, conventional publications do not. But this atomises cultural discussion, to the detriment of the wider public sphere. Those who want to join the arena for, say, performance poetry or the work of minor film-makers or installation artists may well be drawn to relevant websites, but this will disperse the arenas for debate and evaluation. Non-initiates are unlikely to stumble on the relevant sites, which may become, instead, hermetic discussion circles for those already won over to the cause. The danger, again, is that while everybody's interests are catered for, nobody's are challenged or expanded.

The sheer size of the internet is, then, part of this problem. In order for there to be a public sphere, an arena for the wide sharing of ideas and cultural critique, the organs and venues of communication need to be limited. There need to be some voices heard above the din. The number of opportunities the internet provides for criticism and reviewing might seem the opposite of the contraction of academic criticism. But dilation, so far as an arena for public discussion is concerned, is also dilution.

The pullulation of commentary has accompanied a fading of the idea that the critic needs to be a specialist. This is a growing feature of the reception of the arts. Theatre reviewing, for instance, is increasingly undertaken by ex-feature writers or superannuated politicians, figures with an amateur interest rather than a professional association with the theatre. The priorities have shifted towards 'personality' writers with no background in their subject. Authority no longer resides with the professional, since quality is a matter of taste not judgement.

A nomination from Oprah or from Richard and Judy bestows commercial success on a novel far more surely than any other critical response. The huge market that these celebrities can tap is a salutary boon for the book trade, when there are so many other modes of entertainment on offer, and (despite the sniffiness from high-brow quarters) they often choose good books. Yet it attests to the diminution in the role of the critical expert. People will turn to the recommendations of their friends or the celebrities they 'trust'. It seems that a lifetime reading and evaluating novels, plays or films, a mastery of the intricacies of the form and its history, makes one no more qualified to pass judgement on the merits of an artwork than anybody else.

The popular empowerment that the death of the critic superficially mandates has actually led to a dearth of choice. The widening of response has narrowed the possibilities of discrimination. It has facilitated the commercial manoeuvrings of big chain bookstores who heavily promote and advance fewer and fewer titles and authors. Lesser-known writers, perhaps producing vital, innovative work, tend to be swamped out in the commercial din, lacking as they do informed apologists with sufficient authority and access to sufficient numbers of readers. Too often in this arena hype and puff pieces do the work of critical judgement and evaluation. Increasingly, the film industry no longer bothers with previews at all.

For all the supposed emancipation implicit in the pro- nouncement 'we're all critics now', the loss of critical authority, of knowledgeable arbiters with some influence on public attention, actually diminishes the agency and choice of the reader. It plays into the hands of the monopolies who pedal fewer and fewer choices and whose primary interest is always the bottom line. What could be better suited to a ravenously consumerist society, thriving on depthless and instant gratifications, than an ethos where judgements of cultural quality are down to everyone's individual tastes and opinions? Like those phone-in polls so beloved of television and radio, this supposed 'people power' decks out banality and uniformity in the guise of democracy and improvement.

However, in expressing concerns about unexamined, formulaic consumption, let us not try to reinstate dubious hierarchies between high and low culture. To seek excellence and standards of evaluation in professional criticism is not to advocate the return to an age when popular culture was beneath critical notice. The merely popular entertainment of one age becomes the high-brow classic of the next, as the nineteenth-century novel attests. Advocating evaluative criticism is not necessarily to be mandarin and snobbish about popular genres or forms. Hidebound hierarchies are inimical to open-minded evaluation. Quality and standards exist in detective and romance fiction as well as experimental poetry. Arguing for the existence of artistic excellence, and the role of the critic in identifying it, does not mean reintroducing a totem pole of reputable and disreputable art forms. The critic is the enemy of frozen and received wisdoms about artistic value as much as the idea that all such value is ephemeral, relative and simply down to the beholder.

If recent decades have seen television, comic books, musicals and pop music more subject to critical scrutiny and evaluation than hitherto, this is surely to be welcomed. It is inimical to the critical spirit to regard mass entertainments as beneath critical notice. The affording of considerable review space in newspapers and magazines to creative modes previously overlooked as 'low' or 'popular' has released valuable cultural energies into the public space. The career of American film critic Pauline Kael, one of the great post-war critics in the *New Yorker*, often involved subverting supposed hierarchies between art house and mainstream movies: 'one of the surest signs of the Philistine', she remarks, 'is his reverence for the superior tastes of those who put him down' (24). It is more helpful to think of 'dumbing-down' not as a question of what aspect of culture or entertainment gets attention, but of the manner and quality of the criticism it attracts.

In Britain, the broadsheets partly took their cue from the early 1990s magazine the *Modern Review* (1991–95). The *Modern Review* deliberately set out to subject popular culture to serious analysis, billing itself as 'low culture for high brows' as if, in the memorable phrase of one of its founders, Julie Burchill, '*Smash Hits* had been edited by F. R. Leavis'. Such enterprises have demonstrated that taking popular culture seriously, analysing and appraising its relationship to social conditions and, importantly, evaluating its quality can be intellectually and socially enriching. Indeed, critics of popular culture often have an advantage over their more high-brow colleagues. A high-profile figure like Clive James (1939–), who found fame as television critic for the *Observer*, has evaded the elitist, snobbish associations that his peers in more hieratic art forms attracted. Hence, arguably, he could more readily make the transition to media personality. Some of the most notable cultural commentators who work in journalism today began their careers in popular music magazines. These are not figures who censor their passions for fear of condescension. Their cultural evaluations are less freighted with elitist and snobbish associations than the musings of the Brian Sewell, or the Oxbridge dons.

It is, perhaps, to divest themselves of these haughty or superior associations that Oxbridge dons have recently looked askance at the whole business of critical evaluation. A robust recent indictment of the distinctions between high and low culture, and the very notion of value in the arts, is John Carey's *What Good Are the Arts?* Motivated by anti-elitist ardour, Carey, an Oxbridge don himself, assaults the notion that artistic standards can ever exist in any external or 'mystical' realm, maintaining that artistic value is wholly individualist and subjective. It is impossible, he claims, for one artwork to be meaningfully described as 'better' than another. Carey proposes that values, all values not just aesthetic ones, cannot be under-written by any external standards without recourse to some idea of the divine or eternal. Such validation is not available in a non-theistic world, so therefore we cannot see values as having any validity outside the 'person doing the valuing'. Artistic value exists only in people's minds. But the mind of an individual is far too vast and complex a realm for another person to gain access or understanding of it. You cannot, Carey insists, know the mind of another, so you are certainly not in any position to say that your artistic experience (of Wagner) is worthier or better than mine (of Westlife). Art is inescapably personal and cannot be called to account in any objective court. All we can say is, as Carey concludes with satisfaction, 'I don't know much about art but I know what I like' (2005, 31).

I shall treat the substance of Carey's relativism a little later. But his attack on the snobbishness of the defenders of high culture is surely a cat amongst a lot of long-dead pigeons. The privileged idea of high art as a quasi-spiritual beacon of civilization has long been routinely assaulted within and outside the universities. A glance now at Kenneth Clark's era-defining television series *Civilisation* (1966), with its elevation of Western masterpieces and its disdain for popular culture, shows just how alien and dated this sensibility is in the contemporary world. The broadsheet review pages give more space to the latest Hollywood blockbuster than they do to the offerings of the Royal Opera House, which Carey regards as so scandalously pampered and over-sponsored. The process of breaking down high–low distinctions and of disseminating the onus of evaluation to the consumer, which Carey pushes to a logical extreme, had begun decades earlier.

If newspapers and reviewers have given more attention to popular culture in recent years, so too have Humanities departments in universities. 'Cultural Studies' has assumed an important role, not just as an independent discipline but also by its influence on the study of literature and the arts. Differences in the hierarchy between high and low, good or bad, tend to be broken down, often by eschewing the whole question of artistic quality and merit. Texts, artefacts or performances are interpreted and analysed with a view to unlocking the social norms and attitudes encoded therein, not assessed or evaluated as integral, self-contained creations. Cultural studies tends to turn a blind eye to the quality of construction or artistic achievement of its quarry. It aims to deploy criticism for political, not aesthetic, ends, to expose the operations of imperialism, racism or patriarchy. The cultural studies practitioner often suspects any attempt to separate aesthetics from politics as itself a political manoeuvre. Cultural studies, as an academic discipline, may sometimes have had the same object of concern as *Smash Hits* but its approach came with a far more sociological and politicized spin than Leavis would have countenanced in *Smash Hits* or anywhere else.

In many respects, the political turn in the humanities, and the openness it generated in the previously closed-shop of 'Great Literature', has performed a scholarly service that has greatly enriched world culture. Who would not welcome the rediscovery of unjustly forgotten women writers, or the efforts to hear the voices of the marginalized and disempowered which has formed such a significant strand of academic study in recent years? Moreover, cultural studies helped bring history and context firmly back into the frame of consideration. Previous generations of formalists and New Critics had tended to look past the historical period in which a text was set, as if clearing the dust from around sacred hieroglyphics. Not only did they emphasize close reading of 'texts themselves', rather than understanding them in their social moment, but they also tended to see culture and society as merely local accoutrements around a fundamental and unchanging human nature, as if the life experiences of a New York stockbroker, a Medieval serf and an Aztec Indian were essentially the same. In other words, the 'value' of the arts for the formalists and humanist critics was to be found in eternal verities and universal truths about the 'human condition'. It was truths about what-it-is-to-be-alive, rather than alive in a particular place and time, which underwrote the greatness of Shakespeare and Dante.

The emphasis on a 'Great Tradition' and efforts to settle the 'canon' of art and literature that so exercised critics like F. R. Leavis surely needed interrogation. So too did the widespread humanist assumptions that the values and outlooks of Western culture represented a timeless, transcendent human condition. But the response of the succeeding generation, in thrall to a principle of radicalism, was to repudiate or ignore the idea of aesthetic value altogether. Ideas of excellence or standards within the arts seemed irrelevant, dilettantish or even complicit in the silencing of marginalized voices in society. Value judgements, it was insisted, were cultural and artificial, not intrinsic to the objects themselves. In the universities, the battle against 'discrimination' in the negative, racist or sexist sense often had as an early casualty 'discrimination' in the sense of evaluative judgement or discernment.

It was necessary to open up the canon of 'Great Art', to

have an amnesty on the idea of objective quality, in order to allow access to those marginalized voices that had been kept out of it. The criteria for admission needed to be renovated as well as the canon itself with, for example, more recognition for non-traditional literary forms like diaries and letters. It is enriching not only politically, but also aesthetically, to hear those excluded voices, to see how the boundaries of form and convention have been pushed and appropriated. In so far as it renders the issue of quality and merit hierarchically settled, an inflexible, sclerotic canon is, in many ways, as antithetical to evaluation as none at all. The canon should be plastic and pliable, since 'quality' is not an eternal and unchanging facility, but rather one that mutates along with the cultural evolution of a society.

It is an entirely different proposition, however, to do away with the idea of quality and canonicity altogether in the name of inclusivity and political plurality. Unfortunately, however, the cultural studies emphasis tended either to ignore or else be actively hostile to the question of literary or formal 'value' or 'evaluation'. The hostility came from the idea that 'canon-formation' was rigged in favour of the powerful and privileged at the expense of all the dumped and disregarded voices which were so resoundingly absent from the received traditions of literature and culture. However commendable and necessary it might have been to correct some of the exclusions of the traditional canon, the political emphasis had a secondary, less desirable effect. The question in which the reading public would have taken a primary interest – 'Is this book/artwork worth my attention and my time? Is it of any merit?' – was not one that exercised the cultural theoretician.

It was, then, necessary and fruitful for history and context to be returned to the study and criticism of literature. To ignore the social and political aspects of a poem in order to dote over a dactyl can often be to impoverish it. However, with the embrace of inter-disciplinary study the movement often happened in the opposite direction. It was not history that was brought to the arts, a manoeuvre that gives them new and rich significance, but the arts that were brought, subserviently, to history. The social tensions and troubled context of the early seventeenth century were not invoked to help us understand and appreciate Jacobean drama, but Jacobean drama was deployed to help us understand the power dynamics of the seventeenth century. Interdisciplinarity, at its best, means a strategic deployment of politics, history, sociology or philosophy in order to better approach the object of study, that object in the case of English studies being literature. But often the result has been that English has simply been an outpost of other disciplines. Since it downgraded the significance of its own subject matter, English was just an exotic or 'soft' way to do social or political history, heavily coloured by Marxist techniques of uncovering the ideological tensions in the texts under consideration. It was an approach that had an enduring influence on the array of politicized literary critical theories that flourished in the universities since the 1970s from feminism to ethnic studies to post-colonialism.

During this period, then, English studies could be seen to have suffered from the 'Ratner effect', after the notorious gaffe by the jewellery tycoon who publicly sneered at the quality of his company's products and subsequently saw his profits slump. Nobody was more eager to downplay the significance of literature than its own professors and professional practitioners. In its urge to be socially and politically relevant, and in its embarrassment about its own erstwhile elitism, English Studies had punctured its own disciplinary integrity. When a leading critic like John Carey declares 'what critics think about this or that artwork ... is necessarily only of limited and personal interest', we are surely in the realm of the Ratner effect (2005, 167). If critics are saying this about criticism, then should we be surprised if the public lose interest?

The academic and social developments that led to this situation explain, in part, the plunge in the public reputation of academic criticism. One of the few arenas where academics have appeared between the covers of a book read by a wide, non-specialist audience are the 'Introductions' to issues of classical novels. But even this slender outlet seems to be under pressure. Vintage are launching a new series of classical novels to rival Penguin, but they have decided to use journalists and novelists, not academics, to write the 'Introductions'. This is indicative of contemporary attitudes to academic expertise in literature. Could the disciplinary changes in English, in particular the turn from evaluation, partly explain these attitudes?

English professors in the UK and America showed themselves all too eager to transcend the parasitical associations of their calling, to get a chance at writing socially relevant work. At a time when the arts and the universities were under attack by a Thatcherite ideology, which demanded that education prove its worth in the marketplace, English was, unfortunately, showing strong signs of sheepishness and embarrassment about its own relevance. The right-wing economic utilitarianism was all too often faced down with a left-wing political utilitarianism, which styled itself as an opposite but was in many ways a covert double. Both held culture to account in a court of utility, both derided the genteel amateurism and fey inefficacy of conventional literary study. The left-wing literary theorist Terry Eagleton once wondered whether, in an age of economic crisis and nuclear proliferation, we really need another scholarly study of George Crabbe. But the question could equally have been asked by his foes on the Right.

English and the Fine Arts could not help looking enviously at the slick social glamour of cultural studies, with its *engagé* air of political commitment. The very word 'literature' accrued a bad political odour precisely because of its association with the traditionally esteemed. In his hugely influential primer *Literary Theory: An Introduction*, Eagleton pronounces that 'Anything can be literature, and anything which is regarded as unalterably and unquestionably literature – Shakespeare, for example – can cease to be literature' (1983, 10). Academic monographs and anthologies began to replace 'literature' with 'writing', a word without the same undesirable inflection of evaluative prejudice. The change highlighted the voguishness and contemporaneity of these books, at the same time as implying that they strove to document a social group or historical period, not to pass judgement on cultural quality or merit.

But treating literature as social document, though it momentarily gives critics the more primary aura of the social historian, undermines the disciplinary ground on which they work. Why have specialized literature departments? Why not just turn them all into 'cultural' studies without implying any greater value in the canonical than the non-canonical? The problem is, though, that if 'literature' departs, then it takes the 'literary' critic with it, leaving instead a sociologist or cultural theorist at the margins of a borrowed discipline. Without a 'point' to literary studies, without a self-justification, it became no longer even a parasite on literature and art (on the 'real thing') but rather the poor handmaiden of other disciplines. It ceased to be the end and became rather the means, an instrument of academic enquiry rather than an object of it. Little wonder then why, in an age, paradoxically, of burgeoning students of English at university, lovers of literature or a public curious for literary enlightenment would overlook the output of literary academia.

It is telling that critics who did evaluate, and maintained a sense of esteem for the literary creativity, figures like Denis Donoghue, George Steiner or Helen Vendler, maintained a strong non-academic readership. But, in general, academic connections with a wider literate public outside the Ivory Tower became less authoritative during this period. The subversion of the distinction between popular and high arts, which cultural studies advanced, could have boosted the public market for critical books. What prevented this from happening was that both high and low culture tended to be studied in universities in an essentially instrumental way. It sought to make assertions about underlying social context, avoiding impressionistic and loaded questions of quality or creative achievement, questions applicable to popular as much as conventionally 'high' culture. This elision was one factor for the dwindling of popular interest in academic writings on culture. At precisely the time when the syllabi were becoming more culturally inclusive, the academic study of the humanities became more cloistered and insular, relying ever more on its own specialized and forbidding theoretical vocabulary, to the increasing indifference and perplexity of a wider public.

The various Marxist-influenced strands within literary theory emphasize the historical location of artworks, but of course these movements can themselves be historicized and understood in terms of their own cultural moment. The most obvious thing to say about the disparate figures who forged cultural and literary theoretical discussion in the humanities in

Britain and American – Raymond Williams, Roland Barthes, Michel Foucault, Frederic Jameson – is that they wrote their most important works in a period of social revolution: it was an age of civil rights and student insurgency, anti-Vietnam and nuclear disarmament campaigns, the emergence of the women's movement and gay rights. Popular culture and the idea of a youth culture challenged social hierarchy and deference. It was an era marked by its anti-authoritarianism and non-conformism.

This historical current emerges in the tendency to prize radicalism, not only in the overtly political sense, but also in its impetus to pull away and unmask the spurious workings of the most deeply set habits of thought and conception, to challenge assumptions root and branch. In the case of French post-structuralist theorists like Derrida and Lacan this impelled them to expose the foundational premises of Western metaphysics. The thread that made up the whole fabric of Western thought needed, for them, to be unravelled. In the case of post-structuralism, this thread was language. Alongside the more overtly political and materialist movements, modern literary studies has been hugely influenced by the French linguistic philosophies behind structuralism and deconstruction. But even if these movements do not declare any overt political allegiances, not least because the scepticism to which they subscribe instinctively repudiates preset agendas or allegiances, they are nonetheless informed by this ethic of radicalism. They seek to critique the very pith and core of the structures lurking in language, and then to critique the possibility of critique.

While the New Critics specialized in close-reading of the text itself, as opposed to the author's intention or historical background, they were nonetheless inclined towards integration, towards an elucidation of how the artefact as a whole worked. They could then proceed to assess and evaluate the aesthetic effect of these combined parts. One of the best-known new critical studies of poetry, Cleanth Brooks's *The Well-Wrought Urn* (1956), indicates in its title this holistic preoccupation. By contrast the linguistic approach of the post-structuralist movement is much more concerned with analysis than with synthesis, with an artwork's hidden divisions rather than its aesthetic integrity. The word deconstruction (associated with post-structuralism) implies a procedure geared towards the dismantling of the object of study, revealing its fissures and contradictions, its ghostly reliance on the deferred systems of language, not a consideration of the effects of the entirety. It pits itself against the illusions of totality.

The relationship between the linguistic and the more overtly political emphases in literary studies is complicated. They sometimes adopt positions of antagonism against each other, but there is also a large amount of overlap and influence. So, for instance, feminist and post-colonial theories have been heavily influenced by Derridean deconstruction. What they share, though, is an informing ethic of the radical, a belief that intellectual inquiry needs to challenge prevailing assumptions root and branch, that the veils of culture need to be stripped away to understand its underlying workings. As such, both linguistic and political theory were particularly sceptical of any aura of mystery or mystification, the whiff of the 'sacred' that had become attached to literature and the arts since the eighteenth century. Such scrutiny had, unsurprisingly, little reverence for traditional concepts of aesthetic value. Its focus shifted to the workings of textual language as a dismembered system of signification rather than the whole literary artefact. Everything was open to radical critique apart from its own attachment to radicalism, everything should be challenged apart from the urge to iconoclasm, the role of the university theorist was one of dissent from everything, apart from the imperative to dissent.

Little wonder in this environment that concepts like beauty or imagination would be swept aside by a system of inquiry that doubted even the existence of the human subject. When aesthetic or literary value was addressed, it was usually to show the naïve, mystified or politically reactionary context which shaped it. Repeatedly since the 1970s, critics and theorists have rushed to point out that aesthetic value is *constructed* and in no way 'natural' or intrinsic. Eighteenth-century aestheticians may be fond of finding timeless, divine shafts of illumination in the masterpieces of Western culture, but this illusion withers under the sceptical, relativist eye of many modern commentators.

However, to historicize aesthetic value, to recognize it as determined within society not beyond it, does not reveal it as a will-o'-the-wisp, to be torn away from the more quasi-scientific, linguistic objects of enquiry. To recognize that beauty is an invention of human culture is not the end of aesthetics but its beginning. *All* values, ethical as well as aesthetic, may be socially produced, but that does not make them expendable. Furthermore, academic enquiry is saturated in value judgements of one sort or another, even when it is ostensibly value-free. The decision to be impartial or to dispense with interested analysis is itself an evaluative decision, one which implicitly holds up value-free procedures as *better* than evaluative ones.

Literature professors who are sceptical about the idea of literary value still mark their students' exams, and offer advice on how to write eloquent essays. When a teacher urges a pupil to avoid cliché, it is not to find some pure, timeless mode of good writing, it is precisely to learn sensitivity to the cultural and historical location of language to sense when and where it is stale and when fresh. This is just one mundane example of the fact that even if literary quality is embedded in the specifics of time and place, this does not make it random or a simple question of personal taste. That values derive from culture makes them, perhaps, more elusive and harder to ground than the laws of physics, but it does not make them unreal. Though many specialists in ethics recognize that ethical values are 'constituted' by human culture, this does not lead them inexorably to the conclusion that ethical judgements are simply random or in the 'eye of the beholder'.

III

From the earliest days of the university study of English, there was a distrust of individual response as a yardstick for measuring quality – it smacked of the slack and frivolous, not the academically rigorous discipline that the founders of university English were trying to forge. This is one of the reasons why an 'objective' and external canon was sought, rather than a more plastic and mutating one. But supplanting the idea that artistic worth is an intrinsic, timeless property of something with the idea that all aesthetic value is chimerical, random, and relative creates a false opposition in aesthetics as much as it does in ethics. The space between these two extremes is the arena where the whole of modern philosophies of value – ethics and aesthetics – has operated.

This is not to say that evaluative approaches are simply one thing. As the next chapter shall consider, views about what constitutes the 'value' of art, and hence the purpose of criticism, are various and have mutated throughout the centuries along with the prejudices, assumptions and ideologies of the period. Artistic values, like all values, are culturally mediated. John Carey ignores this mediation when he argues that artistic values are no more than a question of personal preference. His position is based on a false opposition. Since 'intrinsic' values cannot exist without divine underwriting, then all values, he argues, are wholly down to what you and I happen to like or dislike. Yet, again, we return to an excluded middle, as if the only choice was between absolute values or personal ones. There is no room in Carey's analysis for the constitutive power of culture. The social and cultural attitudes and ideologies in which we are all, inevitably, steeped and pickled are, for him, more like an external coating or film we can put on or discard at will.

But culture, precedent, history, tradition and the shared judgement of individuals across the ages impinge both on the objects of aesthetic judgement and also, crucially, on our evaluative criteria. Our individual taste does not operate in a vacuum. Civilization is not like a restaurant that we have walked into, where we can peruse the menu at will. We are born into and formed by it. If values are not God-given, this does not instantly mean that they are simply personal. People live their lives in societies, which are themselves made up of families, classes, groups, communities. These communal experiences profoundly effect the tastes, judgements, preferences, assumptions and *values* of individuals.

Carey seems to share with Margaret Thatcher not just her hostility to artistic elitism, but also her notorious declaration that there is no such thing as 'society'. Even if there is no transcendental or divine grounding for our values, culture (in its societal not its artistic sense) thickens the atmosphere in which such judgements are made, prevents them from being mere random elections. Value judgements – unlike statements of fact – may have a subjective dimension, but this does not make them a matter of whim. Values may be relative but this does not make them random.

If it were otherwise our ethical life – which we are less content to devolve to the 'eye of the beholder' – would be intolerable. Carey holds that *all* value judgements (ethical as well as aesthetic) adhere in the person doing the valuing rather than in any objective quality in a situation. Just as something is not 'beautiful' for all time and in all places, nor is something 'good'. Once 'belief in a God is removed', Carey claims, 'moral questions, like aesthetic questions, become endlessly disputable' (2005, 172). To prove his point, Carey cites disagreements over contentious moral issues like the death penalty and abortion.

But, apart from these disputes, there is a great deal of moral consensus in our society. Most of us agree that it is not right or just to cause unnecessary suffering to others, to exploit or neglect the weak, to interfere with basic freedoms, to neglect the poor and old. So too, it is worth pointing out, there is a considerable amount of aesthetic consensus, even if individual responses to artworks vary. But Carey's thesis on value is signally inadequate to underpin any more ambitious challenges to this consensus. Armed with these tools, how could he answer the question that W. H. Auden poses, 'If, as I am convinced, the Nazis are wrong and we are right, what is it that validates our values and invalidates theirs?' If we cannot appeal to some shared sense or cultural grounding that one artwork is better than another, then nor can we say that one moral choice is better than another. There is surely more of a basis for our ethical elections that this.

Of course ethics are disputable. Of course they change in different societies and contexts. We no longer believe in the ethics of witch-burning or in putting the mentally ill on public display. Ethical values, like aesthetic ones, are culturally contingent. But we do not proceed from this recognition to render them the preserve of individual choice. That ethical values have historically been used for dubious political purposes does not now inspire us to jettison the realm of ethics altogether. Imagine if someone summed up ethical values in the way Carey defined aesthetic ones: 'A work of art is anything that anyone has ever considered a work of art, though it may be a work of art only for that one person' (29).

For Carey, the only leverage we have is subjective persuasion. He allows that the bombing of the World Trade Center could, indeed, be a work of art for the composer Karlheinz Stockhausen (who so described it) though he finds it abhorrent. But could the attack that day not be morally 'right', since it was for the people who carried it out and clearly for many others? How would Carey go about refuting them on moral grounds, since the only tool that can be deployed in the realm of value judgements is the rather watery idea of personal opinion?

The only way we persuade is with evidence and evidence has to have an *external* validity. This is not to say that values are 'absolute' or 'intrinsic', but it is to say that they the weight of history, culture, human consensus and intellectual enquiry is far heavier than Carey would allow. However tainted with barbarity 'civilization' has often been at its worst, it determines the trajectory of our moral, ethical and aesthetical judgements. The word T. S. Eliot would use to describe this authority in the aesthetic realm is 'tradition'. Perhaps the only grounding our values have is in the accretions of cultural precedent, a position many philosophers hold. But this is far from Carey's radical subjectivism.

The point is, however, that even if the relativists are right and values are all culturally derived, they do not by that token become immediately expendable or whimsical. It is easy to treat aesthetics this way because, in comparison with ethics, the stakes seem so low. Even the most pronounced moral relativist tends not to be cavalier in ethical principles and practices. The values may be cultural, not eternal, but this is no licence for amorality or immorality. It need not make one person's right and wrong as good as another person's. We can and must choose how much to *value* the variety of values that individual people hold. And we can discriminate amongst them. In the last 30 years, in deconstruction and linguistic philosophy, we have had exhaustive investigations into the meaning of meaning. Perhaps it is now time to devote attention to the value of value.

Treating aesthetic values as, at best, chimerical and personal or, at worst, as politically noxious has become widespread in the study of literature in universities. This treatment, I would argue, has been to the detriment of those mutually enriching connections between Ivory Tower and Grub Street, academic and journalistic criticism. However, I should emphasize that I am not laying the charge for the death of the public critic simply at the door of 'theory'. Throughout the convulsions that have run through the study of the humanities in the last 30 years there have been regular broadsides and blasts against 'theory' as if it was a singular entity that had, lamentably, overrun the academic study of the arts like weeds in a garden. Too often theory is presented by its detractors as a homogeneous and intrusive abstraction that 'gets in the way' of the proper business of criticism. The theorists are surely right in their claim that how we read and how we criticize is a not a neutral, value-free business, and that those who claim to be without a theory are simply in the grip of an older and unacknowledged one. Certainly the post-war flowering of literary criticism had a theory behind it. It was accompanied by a principled agenda for what criticism should be – close attention to form and the words on the page in line with the values of New Criticism. Literary criticism is not like kissing – think about it too much and you're sure to get it wrong – it often demands a methodological self-awareness. The best criticism often pauses to reflect on what it can or should be doing, as well as simply doing it.

Neither the idea that theory gets 'in the way' of real criticism nor the notion that it is too recondite and specialized are enough to explain the dearth of public criticism. The key cause, as I have been arguing, is at once more obvious and more difficult. The democratization of objective critical standards may have partly derived from the anti-authoritarian, anti-hierarchical cultural currents of the 1960s and 1970s. But the disdain for authority, the scorn for mystique, the idea that the proper role of the critic is to penetrate the mystifications of culture, pulling away the veils of the sacred, has also led to a shift away from the notion that the professional critic's job has much to do with evaluation. The constriction of academic criticism may seem in opposition to the dilation of reviewing, but both have assigned judgements of aesthetic quality to subjective response, outside the remit of intellectual scrutiny and inaccessible to any shared gauge or standard.

While in some respects modern theory departs from the concern with literary greatness among the Leavisites, there is an important sense in which suspicion of evaluation and response is as old as the discipline of university English studies. Those who want to imbue the study of the arts with scholarly and empirical rigour have, since early in the twentieth century, long disdained the belletristic connotations of 'appreciation' or 'response'. This is why, for figures like Richards, Eliot and Leavis, debates about merit or quality needed to be toughened into a question of objective standards. There was an institutional as well as an ideological necessity here if English Literature was going to be a respectable university subject, capable of combating accusations of softness and effeminacy.

It was precisely to counter these notions that the practical criticism of I. A. Richards, with its attention to close, muscular reading of words on the page, was initiated. And even if Eliot, Leavis et al. were interested in the concept of literary value in trying to settle on a literary canon or a Great Tradition, it was certainly not to open the door to anything as slack as a response-based, evaluative criticism. Eliot emphasized unsentimental concepts like impersonality and the objective correlative in his criticism. If they were trying to discover a tradition in literary history worthy of serious study, it was to settle the issue of the canon. Not to protract the discussion.

In so far as it tries to settle evaluative processes through the erection of stable canonical hierarchies, the older generation of criticism pits itself against evaluative criticism as much as the younger. In many ways the continuities between literary studies before and after 1968 are as striking as the changes, for all the revolutionary fervour. For Leavis (as for Matthew Arnold) the point of literary studies was the nurture of the moral imagination. Literary success, particularly in the novel, resided in cultivating and celebrating the 'spontaneous-creative life'. In one sense the turn away from literary judgement has been a move from a concern with morality to a concern with politics. But the ethical principles in both beliefs have much in common. One proclaims that a canon of 'Great Works' celebrates culture and cultivation, expanding the moral sensibility of those who encounter it. The other thinks that dismantling the canon and rigid notions of literary merit advances political emancipation and raises social consciousness.

So the two periods have much in common. Analysing and unstitching the obscured continuities pre- and post-1968 reveals that the seeds which destroyed the public critic were planted in the preceding generation, the supposed 'golden age'. In particular, the turn from evaluation in the academic study of English literature precisely lies in the strong emphasis on the 'canon' by the new critics of the 1950s. Deciding on the canon was, after all, meant to settle the issue, to identify the 'Great Works' in a permanent hierarchy, ready for the attentions of a muscular formalist criticism based on close-reading and scrupulous attention to the text. Once frozen, the canon was easily dismantled by the next generation of politicized critics, suspicious of the category of literature as a whole. The refusal of the literary 'canon' may in one respect be an admirably democratic dismantling of fusty old edifices. However, in failing to replace the permanent tradition with any renovated notion of literary merit, in ousting evaluation for simple analysis, criticism has undermined its own disciplinary foundations. This, crucially, is one of the key factors in cutting academic criticism off from a wider reading public.

It is often now said that 'theory' is dead or has been so assimilated into literary studies that the debates of ten and 20 years ago are now obsolete. There have been signs of change in recent years, some of which I will consider in Chapter 4. The theoretical wars of the 1980s and 1990s have cooled, and many of the arguments advanced by theory have been absorbed into mainstream literary critical practice. Part of this is evidenced by the renewed interest in the canonical novel as a source both of moral and psychological insight and aesthetic eloquence.

As the political turn in literary studies becomes absorbed, it is time to interrogate the question of literary and cultural values. Where are they grounded and what do they mean? What underlies the aesthetic achievement of a work of art? Can we meaningfully say that one is better than another? What can 'value theory', a burgeoning area of philosophy, tell us about artistic merit? Only by reconnecting with evaluative approaches will academic criticism tap into the wider public interest in literature and the arts and contribute to a non-academic cultural field.

CHAPTER TWO

The Foundations of Critical Value

I

An early and still-abiding sense of the word 'critic' in English is one who carps, complains or back-bites. The *Oxford English Dictionary* gives this as the primary meaning, while listing the more judicious, impartial evaluation of the professional critic as the secondary one. This association with censure and negativity probably feeds into the pejorative associations of the critic as nay-sayer and ne-er-do-weller. Thomas Dekker in *News from Hell* (1608) combines them: 'Take heed of criticks: they bite, like fish, at anything, especially at bookes'. It would not be hard to fill the pages of this book with quotations vilifying reviewers and critics. Their trade is evaluative hierarchies, but as already seen in Chapter 1, they are low on the totem pole of the writing profession. Though this contempt pre-dates the death of the critic, it perhaps underlies the conspicuous lack of mourning.

A lexicographer might also point at 'critical', describing a grave emergency and 'critique', a mode of philosophical enquiry. The etymological roots are deep and complex but the earliest traceable origin, the Greek word *kritos*, meaning 'a judge', has endured. Professional criticism has for a long time meant much more than simply passing judgement. It also implies explanation, commentary, summary, analysis, interpretation, de-coding and so on. Just as scholarly researchers and interpretative explicators co-exist in university departments of English so, at a certain point in its history, the meaning of 'criticism' merged with the notion of 'exegesis', scriptural explication and interpretation, long-established in the Judeo-Christian scholarly tradition. Therefore as well as judgement and evaluation, criticism can mean reflection or commentary upon arts, crafts, music, architecture or any of the other productions of human creativity, including, of course, the criticism of criticism itself.

One important feature of criticism is its habit of considering its own proper agency and purpose, doubling back on itself to ask the question what it is or should be doing. This means that not only does criticism snap at other people, it can also readily turn around and bite its own tail. Criticism has theory running through its veins, much more so than many of the refuseniks of modern 'Theory' might like to think. This is one of the reasons that criticism boomed in the eighteenth century, around the same time as the new discipline of 'aesthetics' or a philosophy of beauty started to develop in Europe. But even apart from when it explicitly theorizes about itself, all criticism involves a set of attitudes and beliefs, often unarticulated, about the purposes of art and the criteria against which it should be judged. Inevitably, all practising critics reproduce the values, beliefs and ideologies of the society or culture in which they work.

The history of criticism reveals two conflicting impulses: on the one hand, a yearning for stable foundations against which to evaluate (for hundreds of years these were grounded in the classical criteria elaborated by Aristotle and Horace); on the other, a need to accommodate the values of the particular, the sense that art often changed and diversified and needed to be judged against new standards. Often, in practice, a choice emerges: to defend old standards, values and hierarchies against new ones or to defend the new against the old.

A caveat is necessary at this point. Writing a history of criticism that would withstand all theoretical scrutiny is impossible. A history, especially a broad one like this, involves narrative organization of some kind, a selection based on what seems important retrospectively, emphasizing supposed con-tinuities and contrasts, chronological and logical organization, which are all to a large extent impositions from the present. In other words recasting the ragged multifarious past of criticism, with all its loose ends and dead ends, into a coherent narrative is to be guilty of precisely the sort of naïve realism that much contemporary cultural theory would revile.

But much of the discipline of history (which needs to shape the loose, chaotic complexity of the recorded past into neat narrative form, with beginning and end, cause and effect) could be subject to the same attack. Like the historian, I can only plead that this broad-brush history of attitudes towards artistic value is not proposing that criticism has an essential sameness. What the story shows is precisely how disrupted and fluctuating the function and practice of criticism has been, how responsive to a society's notion about the point or purpose of art, even when, as in the later nineteenth century, the point of art was its glorious pointlessness. Commentary on art and literature makes value judgements all the time. That, at various moments in the twentieth century, the proper role for the critic was held up to be 'disinterestedness', not allowing personal partiality to colour judgement, is itself a evaluative stance, though one which favours the value free.

Criticism, if it is a handmaiden of art, also calls it to account, addresses what it is for and, relatedly, what is its proper mode of expression. This is why the deepest roots of criticism actually lie in literature itself. All written forms double back and ponder their own purpose. The earliest literature often includes self-critique, when the poet ponders on the significance and direction of the story he is telling or calls upon the Muse to safely guide his voice or pen to an accurate or worthy representation. Even Homer sometimes reflects on where poetic inspiration comes from and where lies its proper subject, form and purpose. The roots of literary criticism are to be found in this tendency, which pre-dates the usual starting point for histories of Western criticism in Greek philosophy (though Indian 'Vedic' criticism may have influenced the Greeks). However, the conventional history of criticism usually turns to Plato and Aristotle as the earliest to develop literary and artistic principles within self-contained *non*-literary works.

The still-strained relationship between the critic and the artist got off to a notoriously bad start. Plato's critical reflections led him to advocate the banishment of artists from his ideal Republic. Since poets pedal in imitations and fictions, they threaten to distract citizens from their duties to the state, deflecting their minds from its proper object, ideal truth. Plato depicted the physical world as merely a ghostly echo of perfect celestial ideas. The perception of a tree or a table, then, is merely a flickering approximation of the perfect forms of these things, merely a copy. The arts are at one further remove: a copy or imitation of this imperfect copy. Therefore, for Plato, poetry and the arts enchant the citizen away from truth and virtue, towards delusion and passion. Though he was attuned to the great allure of the arts, it is philosophy, not poetry, which brings us close to the real essence of things for him. If Plato anticipates the modern antagonism between the 'creative' and the 'critical', what he calls in *The Republic* 'the ancient feud between poetry and philosophy', coming down on the side of the latter, he also inaugurates the long and complex intersection between evaluative criticism and ideas of the *moral* and the *true*. Over the ensuing centuries, critics would often orbit their judgements around these two pillars, praising or condemning artworks for inculcating virtue and vice in one long tradition, or for reaching or falling short of veracity in another. Since at different moments and at different levels of emphasis, these are two of the purposes of art – revealing to us some truth about the world or making us better people – these are the criteria which critics have often used for measuring artistic merit. For Plato, art, despite its tremendous power and appeal, failed on both counts and thus was forfeit.

The idea that an artwork is corrupting, misleading or irreligious would motivate many a censorship campaign in the ensuing centuries. But even modern critics who indict an artwork for its politically noxious message – alleging anti-Semitism in Shakespeare's *The Merchant of Venice* or a domineering male gaze in Fragonard's *Bathers* – are judging these artworks against venerable criteria of morality and the social good. It may be that these days the detected corruption comes from existing authority, rather than pitted subversively against it, but the court in both cases is an ethical one.

Literary criticism, for Plato and the Greeks, is inherently pedagogic and didactic. It provides guidance for what citizens should read and think by constraining the wayward, visionary, polymorphous aspects of poetry and the arts. Happily Plato's successors came up with less exilic prescriptions for the poets and artists. Aristotle also asserts the moral and social importance, but counters Plato by espousing the psychological benefits. While Plato sees art as dangerously inflammatory of the human emotions, Aristotle thinks that it can satisfy and regulate them. Poetry and drama does not just imitate objects, hence making them less real. It also imitates 'noble actions' and this can have a salutary effect on spectators. In his *Poetics* Aristotle offers an attempt to define 'tragedy', which he praises as the highest of the literary forms. In possibly the most often quoted passage in the history of criticism, he defines tragedy as 'an imitation of an action that is admirable, complete and possesses magnitude' that seeks to effect through 'pity and fear the purification of such emotions' (1996, 10). Aristotle's notion of the catharsis of pity and fear steers the emphasis onto the beneficial mental effects on the spectators of a tragic drama, removing thereby ('catharsis') the disruptive toxins of 'pity' and 'fear' from the body politic.

Again, we can detect variations on this foundational Aristotelian theme in the following centuries. It would be particularly influential in theories of that most contentious and oft-considered of genres, tragedy. But emphasis on psychology of the spectator, and its social effects, would be a key strand in the history of criticism as a whole. The notion that art is 'good for you', that it can operate as a sort of an enema for the soul, cleansing negative, despondent feelings or violent emotions, is one that has endured. It has had a particularly strong currency among twentieth-century psycho-analytical theorists. But the literature-as-therapy model, the notion that books raise or inspire the spirit, also underlies the assumptions about the value of reading in, for instance, Oprah's book club.

Aristotle's work, though frequently held up by the neo-classicists as a blueprint of how things ought to be done, was more descriptive than prescriptive, based as it was on his own exposure to performances of dramatic tragedies, especially those of Sophocles. Nevertheless much ancient criticism, such as that of Horace, Cicero and Quintillan in Rome, was absorbed in technical rules and advice to aspiring writers. Horace extends and amplifies Aristotle's categorization of literary forms to include lyric, satire, elegy and epigram, as well as epic, tragedy and comedy. His *The Art of Poetry* was to influence Dryden, Johnson and Pope amongst many others, though he is also celebrated as a key inaugurator and explicator of the genre of satire. The controlled, taxonomic, rational way of approaching artistic forms in which Horace excelled appealed to the critics of the seventeenth and eighteenth centuries, as did Horatian 'common sense', his humour and his tone of educated reason.

Two further figures from Antiquity should be mentioned: Plotinus and Longinus. If Plato saw art as imitative and Aristotle as psychological, then the neo-Platonist philosopher Plotinus regarded it as spiritual. Art did not simply imitate nature (which was, for Plato, an imitation of the true transcendent ideas, mere flickerings on a cave wall): it has itself direct access to the true world of forms. So, rather than being at one further remove from truth, the artist goes back to the pure ideas from which nature derives. Therefore artistic beauty provides an independent route to spiritual enlightenment.

Longinus (who wrote in Greek, but may have been Roman) is another key figure in theories of artistic effect. His idea of the 'sublime' elevated the effect of art beyond any formal conventions or predictable responses. He describes the sublime (*hypsous*) as 'a certain high excellence of expression by virtue of which the greatest writers of prose and poetry have achieved pre-eminence and timeless recognition'. The sublime finds a harmonious combination between the intellect (*noesis*) and the emotions (*pathos*). Against the rhetoricians of his day, or the decorous, harmonious categories of Horace, Longinus recognized a more wayward, less biddable idea of artistic value. The sublime is the transcendent element that transmutes an artistic work into more than the sum of its parts. The sublime was treated variously by eighteenth-century aestheticians and thinkers, most famously (though with significant differences between the two) by Kant and Burke. In distinction to the order, reason and harmony of the beautiful, the sublime was terrifying, awe-inspiring, dangerous. It was the germ for the influential idea that art accesses truths beyond the rationally articulable. The sublime has had a more recent fluorescence in a number of theorists such as Paul de Man and Jean-François Lyotard, not least because it seems to challenge the knowable and rational, revealing the inadequacies of our conceptual powers and the instabilities of the postmodern world.

Criticism, as I have been arguing, is inextricably associated with shifting values, not just the value judgements it makes about individual works – are they 'good' or 'bad'? – but the criteria or principles upon which such judgements are made, usually notions about the 'effect' or 'purpose' of the arts. In other words, the individual judgements are informed by general ideas about art: the better an artwork serves its purpose (truth, good example, emotional uplift), the better it is. For all the radical shifts and convolutions of the cultural purpose of art, many of the debates and beliefs in the ensuing centuries do evoke the aesthetic values of Plato, Aristotle, Plotinus and Longinus, often in hybridized form. Art is valued or disdained for its moral, social or political impact, for its psychological effects, for its spiritual or quasi-spiritual access to 'truth', for its excellence of composition and the intensity of wonder it provokes. Critical judgement has always orbited around these figurations (and combinations therein) whether the influence of the ancients is explicit or not.

II

The medieval traditions of Christian philosophy, in the work of thinkers like Hugh of St Victor (1078–1141), Bernard of Clairvaux (1090–1153), and above all Thomas Aquinas (1225–74), helped to shape the modern practice of criticism, not least in its concern with interpretation and biblical exegesis. The later middle ages saw Petrarch (1304–74) and Boccaccio (1313–75) combining some of the classical literary principles with medieval moral precepts, but it was the Renaissance, with its rediscovery of antiquity, which opened the floodgates to the classical artistic ideals. Possibly the most influential Renaissance critic was Ludovico Castelvetro (c. 1505–71), whose 1570 commentary on the *Poetics* elaborated on Aristotle's 'unities' of place and time and prescribed tightly structured, rule-based drama. For the next 200 years, critics looked to ancient poems and plays for the permanent laws of art. They provided a standard against which artistic greatness could be gauged, while deviations from this classical norm – as in the adulterated genre of tragicomedy – were often rebuked.

The idea that artistic creativity might be profane or ungodly persisted; Puritan attacks on the theatre were common in the sixteenth century. Sir Philip Sidney's *Defence of Poesie* (1595) famously defends the drama, on moral grounds, against the Puritans, while also complaining about the popular theatre's violations of the permanent aesthetic rules. Within the *Defence*, however, can be discerned the germ of a more modern, less hidebound sense of aesthetic value. So, for instance, Sidney (1554–86) argues for poetry's superiority over history and philosophy, avoiding the arid facts of one and the bloodless abstractions of the other. He also sees it as having a power beyond nature:

> Nature never set forth the earth in so rich tapestry as divers poets have done; neither with so pleasant rivers, fruitful trees, sweet-smelling flowers, nor whatsoever else may make the too much loved earth more lovely. Her world is brazen, the poets only deliver a golden. (1595, 24)

While still honouring the classical forms and the need for poetry to instruct, Sidney's recognition of the power of poetry anticipates the shift towards more self-contained aesthetic value and the idea of beauty as its own avenue to truth that the Romantics will later expound and espouse.

The history of criticism often hinges around a tense polarity between received standards of taste and artistic innovation, objective values and subjective responses, the general and the particular. One needs to have criteria for judgement, especially in a society that values order, reason, harmony, but at the same time art has a way of confounding these criteria. The veneration of the ancients and the insistence on Horatian norms was less insistent in England than in France (Corneille, Voltaire). One reason for this was the presence of Shakespeare (1564–1616), who so magnificently broke the rules but whose greatness could not be gainsaid. The motif of Shakespeare's genius triumphing over formal imperfections can be heard in major British critics from John Dryden (1631–1700) and Alexander Pope (1688–1744) to Samuel Johnson (1709–84).

Dryden, the 'father of English criticism' in Johnson's view, was key in the development of a more pragmatic approach that, while mindful of neo-classical standards, allows room for critical agency and judgement. He disputes the idea, common even in his day, that criticism is negative, primarily about fault-finding: 'they wholly mistake the nature of criticism who think its business is principally to find fault. Criticism, as it was first instituted by Aristotle, was meant a standard of judging well; the chiefest part of which is, to observe those excellencies which should delight a reasonable reader' (I, 179). Dryden judiciously loosened the strictures, recognizing talent that obeys the spirit of the rules while sometimes violating the letter. Good criticism is good judgement, a sense of what will please the common reader (not the last time this concept would be invoked) and an ability not just to say that the literary work pleases, but also to say *why* it does so ('observe those excellencies').

Practising a criticism in which objective principle and precedent would inform but not prescribe or foreclose on the merits of particular artworks was Dryden's great achievement and example. He embodies 'Restoration' values in his resistance to two poles: the rigid authoritarianism of the old monarchy, with its frozen hierarchy of genres on the one hand, and the spurning of all authority in literary judgement, reflecting the lawlessness of the Interregnum, on the other. There are rules, but they are self-imposed ones, limited by their historical context. If, in the twentieth century, criticism has moved from declarations of a timeless and unchanging canon to a postmodern relativism and scepticism about literary value, there is a sense in which Dryden navigated between a comparable Scylla and Charybdis.

The classical standard was an enduring yardstick for

evaluating artworks, a tool that provided the critic with a court of appeal grounded in a verifiable set of criteria. However, it is important to bear in mind that the emphasis on imitating the ancients, far from being a burden on the writers of the time, actually freed them from the obligation to write scriptural and religious allegory. Poets and critics should attend to the classics, the thinking went, because the ancients were the ones who had discovered the rules of nature and established the archetypal and enduring literary genres. As Alexander Pope put it:

> Those rules of old, discover'd, not divised,
> Are Nature still, but Nature methodized;
> Nature, like Liberty, is but restrain'd
> By the same laws which first herself ordain'd.
>
> *Essay on Criticism* (1711), ll. 88–9

In its aphoristic, exquisitely polished rhyming couplets, offering judicious advice to the would-be judge of literature, Pope's *Essay on Criticism* examined not just criteria for art but also criteria for criticism. It is, therefore, a meta-critical exercise, restricting its remarks to critics and criticism and not examining, as Dryden did, the actual literature that had been and was being written. In a sense then, the *Essay on Criticism* is a work of *poetry* (since it is in verse) and a work of *theory* (since it reflects on the purpose of criticism).

As well as offering guidelines for effective criticism, Pope robustly argues for the moral and cultural value of the critic in a civilized society. As such it anticipates other apologias for criticism as a guarantor of civilized values that would later be advanced by intellectuals like Matthew Arnold and T. S. Eliot. Criticism, for Pope, is a means of preserving and ensuring good judgement through fidelity to 'Nature' which, in line with eighteenth-century beliefs and values (at least in the social stratum in which Pope lived and wrote), was as orderly, regulated and wise as one of Pope's own couplets. Poetry, then, did not imitate and distort nature as in the Platonic view. It reproduced the symmetries of natural, divinely designed order in its own textures and forms. Art and Nature became, in this way, happily reconciled, both acting as a harmonious alternative to the fractious and divisive realities of eighteenth-century history. Art did not just represent the appearance of the natural world: it performed the same sort of ordered creations as the natural world. It did not just passively reflect nature; it actively reproduced it. The value of art, then, was not just imitation. It was, as it were, mimicry.

The modern critic was born in the salons and coffee houses of the early eighteenth century. The period saw a rising professional class gain power and wealth, creating a bloc to challenge the traditional monopoly of aristocratic privilege. It was these shifting political structures that created the cultural conditions where a recognizably modern criticism could thrive. The decline in the power and prestige of the court and the growth of a bourgeois 'public sphere' engendered a social conversation of educated people who indulged in urban life and urbane manners, conversation and wit. The development of journals, magazines and periodicals aimed at a literate audience, such as Richard Steele's *Tatler*, Joseph Addison's and Steele's *Spectator* and Samuel Johnson's *Rambler*, inaugurated a vital vehicle for public discourse. Such literary and cultural magazines provided a platform for cultural, social and literary debate and conversation. They were the forum for a new genre of non-fiction prose: the literary and political essay.

The essayists' judgement assumed great importance by the mid-eighteenth century, with the growth of a huge new public eager for informed opinion on culture and the arts. A critical spirit flourished in these conditions. There was an increased scepticism, and an appeal to educated sensibility, cultivated taste, good sense and reason. There was a feeling that consensus was simply a matter of polite persuasion or decorous satire, and the idea took hold that a rational and civilized discourse could be conducted by like-minded people on modern social life, politics and economics, literature and philosophy. These conditions, famously described by the philosopher Jürgen Habermas as the development of the 'public sphere', seemed to bring individuals together in a community with a shared belief in universal reason and the harmony of nature.

All this helped to increase the professionalization of criticism as an enterprise that could direct and inform public taste. The rise of the critic in the eighteenth century, then, came along with the enfranchisement of the middle classes as generators of cultural life. Despite the current, snobbish associations of the critic as mandarin, this early development was an intellectual movement from below, a way of appropriating and redistributing cultural authority from the aristocracy and land-owning classes. As the eighteenth century progressed, the agency of the critics expanded. They were responsible not just for regulating neo-classical decorum but for circulating the civilized values of the society. Alongside these developments was a harder economic basis for the critic. The arts were no longer the preserve of aristocratic patrons and appreciators. The middle classes could purchase paintings, commission designers and architects, and frequent theatre and music concerts. This new paying audience led to a need for an articulation of standards, a need met by critics who would operate, to use Joseph Addison's phrase, as 'arbiters of taste', directing the consumers as to what was valuable in the arts.

The critics of the period were the ciphers for deep cultural questions about the value, the proper function, and the correct techniques and forms of art and literature. These questions were, it was invariably assumed, universal: the standards of taste were the same everywhere and at all times. The rules of poetry seemed to embody the wider social values of balance, judiciousness, clarity, discipline, reason. But these were virtues because they were based on the primary value of 'common sense': the civilized and developed human society operating in accord with the ordered rules of 'Nature'. It was not the rules that made civilization, but rather a harmonious civilization that operated in accordance with these rules. And this harmony needed to be maintained by enlightened and cultivated participants in the public sphere.

III

The eighteenth century was also a period of philosophical reflection. The concept of the critic as a distinct evaluator of the arts developed at the same time as aesthetics emerged from philosophy. The German philosopher Alexander Baumgarten (1714–62) is credited with coining the term 'aesthetics'. He wanted a science of beauty to match ethics, metaphysics and epistemology. British philosophers of the same period – Shaftesbury, Hutcheson, Burke, Kames and Hume – did not adopt Baumgarten's label but they have much to say about ideas of beauty and taste, which were exemplified for these thinkers in both natural and artistic creativity. But their dominant focus for discussion of beauty was often art, not nature.

Lord Kames (1696–1782) was a Scottish judge, who attempted in *Elements of Criticism* (1762) to give criticism a rational groundwork in empiricism and psychology, offering an evaluation of literature and the arts in terms of their capacity to bring to mind an ordered string of passionate responses. Criticism, the cultivation of taste and discernment, edifies and cultivates the individual and society:

> The science of rational criticism tends to improve the heart no less than the understanding. It tends in the first place, to moderate the selfish affections: by sweetening and harmoniz-ing the temper, it is a strong antidote to the turbulence of passion and violence of pursuit: it procures to a man so much mental enjoyment, that in order to be occupied, he is not tempted to deliver up his youth to hunting, gaming, drinking; nor his middle age to ambition; nor his old age to avarice (I: 16).

Admittedly, not every critic since then has lived up to Kames's ideals of moderation and probity. He was typical of his time, however, in believing that cultivation goes in one direction only – that all who are properly educated you will share the same critical judgements. He could therefore regard criticism as a rational pursuit (rather than simply a question of individual proclivity) that could be studied like a science. Kames bases this new science on the belief that he can generalize or universalize his observations of individual psychologies and responses to artworks. It would not be the last attempt to ground criticism on scientific principles. In practice, he defends neo-classical taste based on universal human nature, which he recognizes is upheld only by a small group of people who enjoy leisure, live in an enlightened age, and escape corruption.

Hume's 'On the Standard of Taste' (1757) is more acutely

aware of what will be an abiding problem: that of grounding or justifying standards of artistic quality, given the variety of responses and evaluations among different people. Hume (1711–76) points both at the endurance of a writer like Homer and appeals to the self-evidence that some artists are better than others. He does so in order to argue that taste must be learned and cultivated. Wide exposure to the arts is necessary for the informed and judicious critic though at the same time he argues that the critic needs to approach the artwork without 'prejudice'. The contradiction involved here – that the critic should be a store of previous artistic experience but at the same time assess a work impartially – is not fully resolved. Taste can be learned, there are standards, but there are also responses based on passion and individual feeling. It is arguable that, though he strives to argue for the existence of cultivated 'standards', much of Hume's thinking about the arts allows a relativistic genie out of the bottle.

Sensing the relativism that shadows Hume's approach, Immanuel Kant (1724–1804) wrote his famous *Critique of Judgement* (1790), the most sophisticated theory of aesthetics that had yet been offered and the most influential since the Greeks. What distinguishes the human response to the 'beautiful' from the simple gratification of a desire (like eating and drinking) is its *universal* validity. When someone calls a thing beautiful, he demands the same response from others:

> In all judgements by which we describe anything as beautiful we tolerate no one else being of a different opinion and in taking up this position we do not rest our judgements upon concepts but only on our feeling. Accordingly we introduce this fundamental feeing not as a private feeling but as a public sense. Now, for this purpose, experience cannot be made the ground of this common sense, for the latter is invoked to

justify judgements containing an 'ought'. The assertion is not that every one *will* fall in with our judgement, but rather that every one *ought* to agree with it. (84)

The critic, by implication, does not simply broadcast his own subjective enthusiasms, but rather attempts to persuade his audience of universal truths. Clearly, this philosophy is fundamentally in opposition to the one-opinion-is-as-good-as another/eye-of-the-beholder ethos. We may intuit our artistic understanding subjectively, but we treat beauty 'as if' it were a 'property' of the object. Kant sees significant kinship between aesthetic and moral judgements. Both involve intimations of the divine and demand universal assent. We might gain our experiences of the beautiful subjectively, but a valid aesthetic judgement is a universal one.

Not least of the tremendous influence of Kant's aesthetic philosophy is his emphasis on 'disinterestedness'. Through the idea that the beautiful moves beyond simple subjective desire, Kant established for the aesthetic realm an autonomy among other values. This justified the arts as a distinct area of human activity no longer beholden to moral or political relevance. In its very self-containment and purposelessness, however, art had a more serious and sanctified role, giving us intimations and shafts of illumination of the transcendent and divine world. The individual's sensory experience of the arts moves to a super-sensory experience of the divine.

Henceforward, art's purpose and point moved out from social improvement or the moral instruction of an audience that had so exercised previous theorists. For the Kantians the aesthetic was realized in shuffling off this engagement with day-to-day life, becoming valuable precisely because it was an area of human activity that separated itself from the ordinary, utilitarian world. In other words, paradoxically, the value of art came to be seen more in terms of its 'valuelessness', in so far as it was not something to be put to tawdry purposes or uses. Art becomes, in this, understanding, the direct opposite of propaganda.

This 'disinterested' imperative applies to the critic too. As so often with the shifting values of the arts, an influential credo of artistic value doubles back on to conceptions about the proper role of the critic. In order to activate the beauty in the artwork, the observer or critic needs to be purified of personal and prejudicial concerns. The ideally disinterested critic avoids violating the non-instrumental aura of the artwork. It should not be approached with agendas or prejudices.

The shift in emphasis on the purpose of art did not happen immediately and a didactic role, in which art should improve the moral fibre of the spectator, endured alongside the new 'disinterested' emphasis. Nonetheless, the idea that arts should not be held to mundane or utilitarian account fundamentally coloured the way we routinely think about them, implying that they have a special aura unlike other modes of human practice and human creativity. The belief that artistic value is not just social or psychological or moral has been profoundly tenacious. We see it informing diverse cultural movements, such as the fin-de-siècle aesthetic movement ('art for art's sake') and the modernist espousal of art above the petty concerns of the bourgeois marketplace.

Kant is the most influential figure in concepts of modern aesthetic value. Inevitably his theories were attacked by the cultural theorists in the closing decades of the twentieth century. Ironically, aesthetics was drawing renewed interest in the discipline of philosophy at this period, but in English studies it was typically treated as a bourgeois ideology, a way of obscuring the agendas of privilege behind a veil of disinterested contemplation. The equation of the beautiful with the 'divine' and 'universal' was scorned by critics insistent on the historical location of art, its indelible implication in its own context and social moment. Removing it to the transcendent realm, they would claim, eschews its involvement in political power, obscuring its reinforcement of hierarchical or oppressive ideology by its aura of the religious and the mystical. Such critics point out that, before Kant, the art of pre-industrial and non-Western societies was often collaborative and decorative, without the distinction between the utilitarian and the artistic. They strive to place in its context that key moment in the history of artistic value when the aesthetic was so emphatically moved outside history. Kant's theories of art (and, he confines himself to European art) takes us not just to a universal and timeless realm, but to the drawing rooms and library of God himself.

The growth of aesthetics and the philosophical bases for beauty meant that the criteria for evaluation shifted. The neo-classical ideals, so venerated for so long, no longer seemed necessary to buttress critical judgement. A different sort of art now seemed achievable, one that would access that ineffable, transcendent, or awesome quality of the aesthetic. The concept of art having its own imaginative energy, rather than being based on balanced imitation, heralded the new approach to art and criticism which came to be known as romanticism.

The birth of romanticism swung the pendulum in an opposite direction to neo-classicism. The impetus of neo-classicism came from the prestige of ancient learning; that of romanticism came from connecting to popular cultural forms. Neo-classicism sought to reach the apogee of cultivation and civilization; romanticism celebrated nature and wilderness.

The word 'nature' has very different meanings for the neo-classicists and the Romantics. For the Romantics it had nothing to do with reason and order, but, rather, referred to the non- or pre-civilized world, whose 'natural' forms and organic unity the poet should try to access and emulate. Poetry, for the Romantics, needed to be liberated from imposed rules and the artifice of 'poetic diction'. In the fifteenth century, writing in the vernacular (not Latin) had to be justified by Dante and Boccaccio; now William Wordsworth (1770–1850) and Samuel Taylor Coleridge (1772–1834) wanted to plumb the poetic possibilities of everyday speech, especially that of ordinary, working people.

Romanticism was born in German aesthetic theory and the criticism of figures like Gotthold Ephraim Lessing (1729–81), Friedrich Schiller (1759–1805) and August Wilchem von Schlegel (1767–1845). In England, significantly, the movement's greatest writers were also its most important theorists. Wordsworth's 'Preface' to *Lyrical Ballads* (1800) stressed the 'democratic' aspect of the new movement and advocated the proper language of poetry as language ordinarily used by people (a principle scandalously put into practice in the *Ballads* themselves). Coleridge, who collaborated with Wordsworth on the *Lyrical Ballads*, introduced in his *Biographia Literaria* (1817) perhaps the key concept of English Romantic theory, the importance of the *imagination*. This is the force that yokes together diverse aspects of experience, knowledge and passion into a single unitary vision of the world.

John Keats (1795–1821) did not leave a major critical essay or preface, but he engaged so much with the meaning of poetry in his poems and letters that he has a role in the history of criticism. He advanced the idea of art as 'non-scientific', as opening an avenue to truth outside the empiricist or rationalist emphasis on fact or reason. In terms of the relationship with reality, poetry is more true than mundane, observed experience, because more intensely imaginative. The imagination grasps truth through beauty, which for Keats amounted to the same thing: ' "Beauty is truth, truth beauty" that is all / Ye know on earth and all ye need to know', as he famously puts it in 'Ode on a Grecian Urn' (1884). He emphasized the value of 'negative capability', which he defined as the poetic ability to enter fully into the emotional and intellectual facets of the literary image, to lose one's identity and one's striving after rational coherence so that the senses can feel comfortable in 'uncertainties, Mysteries, doubts, without any irritable reaching after fact & reason' (I, 193). The idea that art can be constitutive of truth, rather than imitating a pre-existing reality, would prove enduringly influential and Keats was a large influence on Wilde and the aesthetic critics of the late nineteenth century. Moreover, the idea that beauty overcomes every other consideration, even the ego or personal identity of the poet, finds an echo in T. S. Eliot's later emphasis on 'impersonality' (see Chapter 3).

As so often in the history of criticism, the Romantics' critical writings went hand in hand with a theory of art's purpose or value. This, in its turn, led to an advocacy of proper theme and form in poetry. Since the Greeks, the arts were regarded as having a keen moral relevance, whether for good or for ill. In the view of the neo-Platonists, they were seen as releasing insubordinate and illegitimate emotions, based on illusion, and hence leading to social instability. In the eighteenth century, art was widely seen as having a responsibility to 'instruct' the reader or spectator, to inculcate virtue and eliminate vice. The censorship activities of many societies imply a view of art and writing as dangerous, subversive and destabilizing.

But it was the Romantics, and particularly Percy Bysshe Shelley (1792–1822), who, adopting this idea, inverted the value judgement inherent in it. He developed the notion that poetry is a radical force for spiritual and social liberation. He sees poetry as, crucially, formative of cultural ideas and social mores rather than just imitative of them. Hence the oft-quoted phrase from his *Defence of Poetry*, written in 1821 but not published until 1840, that poets are the 'unacknowledged legislators of the world'. His defence of poetry is a defence of the fecundity of the imagination. Translated into social and political terms, it becomes a defence of perpetual revolution against hardening or calcifying thought forms. The emphasis and deployment of metaphor in the *Defence* pits it in opposition to dogma and there is no systematic theory. In a sense, Shelley articulates the view of art as a war against cliché, of language or of thought generally. The subversiveness of poetry is its virtue, not its vice.

Romanticism in England, as the case of Shelley exemplifies, was often a pretty left-leaning affair politically, with close connections to the spirit of the French Revolution. However, in another strain of Romanticism, with its cult of the hero and the folk, its belief in primitive energies and its 'blood and soil' ideology, we find the origins of virulent right-wing national-ism. Most obviously, some of the tenets of Nazism have their roots in strands of German Romantic theory. Elevating heroic creativity and exalted beauty means that the sufferings and everyday concerns of the weak and vulnerable can be overlooked. In one development, Romanticism leads to autonomy for art, but in another it can lead to a spillage of artistic values into the political realm, in which rationally ordered and humane principles are overtaken by atavistic forces, anti-individualism and imposed fascistic systems of order. Or, to put it another way, romantic ideology in the public realm can result in the 'aestheticisation of politics', to borrow Walter Benjamin's phrase.

Yet Romanticism in the English tradition is generally free of this taint. The values and beliefs of the English Romantics, with their early valorization of the French Revolution, are geared towards liberationist politics. When Wordsworth advocates a quotidian poetic idiom and theme it is precisely to connect human beings regardless of social rank, Shelley's exaltation of the poetic imagination is geared towards a politics of emancipation. It would be easy to overstate how the veneration of art as valuable through its own intensity and access to non-rational truth has displaced the older notion that art should inculcate virtue. There are often political and social implications in the Romantic defence of art and the imagination. Throughout the history of criticism the two domains, aesthetics and political, the beautiful and the good, persistently dance around each other even when most ostensibly independent.

It is the universal aspirations of aesthetics that often draws most ire from modern theorists. The attempt to define beauty in absolute or trans-cultural terms seems nefarious in the eyes of many modern commentators, schooled in the instability of language or the relativity of values. While, as I have stressed above, criticism often reflects on its own procedures and assumptions, and the development of criticism is closely connected to the growth of the philosophy of aesthetics, it is also the case that the finest critics have often been the least formulaic or systematic.

Criticism needs no common denominator or skeleton key

to unlock aesthetic values, timeless or otherwise. As Walter Pater (1839–94), in the Preface to his *Studies in the History of the Renaissance* (1873), attempts to find some 'universal formula' for beauty, help us little 'to enjoy what has been well done in art and poetry' (xix). Criticism is often geared towards particular instances, close interpretations, diverse practices. Often the best critics are those least exercised with the search for the most abstract and all encompassing definition of artistic value. In order to be open to the new, the critic needs to avoid calcifying his own methods, constraining experience by pre-cooked principle. So the best parts of Coleridge's *Biographia Literaria* are not the passages of aesthetic theorization but the sections treating Wordsworth's poetry, where we see the judicious and discriminating (in the best sense of the word) critic at work, mindful of defects yet generous in praise. The judgements are cool, categorical, penetrating and rational, and always supported with astute reference and quotation.

The Romantic critic who best mastered the art of the particular was William Hazlitt (1778–1830). For Wordsworth and Coleridge, criticism was an offshoot of their poetic endeavours, but Hazlitt made his name principally as an essayist, critic and journalist. He was a radical with a social conscience who fervently supported the French Revolution and Napoleon – even after many of his Romantic contemporaries (like Wordsworth and Coleridge) had become disillusioned and repelled by the violence of both. He made a conscious attempt to formulate what would later be called 'impressionistic criticism':

> My opinions have sometimes been called singular: they are merely sincere. I say what I think: I think what I feel. I cannot

help receiving certain impressions from things; and I have sufficient courage to declare (somewhat abruptly) what they are. This is the only singularity I am conscious of. (v, 175)

The task of criticism, for Hazlitt, is the communication of feelings. As such, what is new in his work is the deployment of brilliant style and partisan tone together with acumen and judgement that often reveal tremendous flair. He has unique powers of description, animated by aphoristic brilliance and fluent capacity to praise or blame virtues or defects in a particular work.

Unlike Coleridge, who could occasionally adopt a bitter tone against the reviewing establishment, Hazlitt earned his living writing for periodicals like the *Examiner* and the *Edinburgh Review*. He faces a new middle-class audience, which he wants to win over, to cajole to the enjoyment of literature. The critic becomes neither a judge nor a theorist, but a partisan and a persuader. He does not appeal to rules or models, theories or systems. His critical works are the record of his own personal response to what he has read and, as such, are remarkably vivid and excited testaments of appreciation. But Hazlitt's was no mere 'quote-and-dote' mode of criticism either; artistic appreciation is not exclusively for the politically indifferent dandies and fops. A lover of art, he recognizes that aesthetic values can both reinforce and resist political power. His is a trenchant but supple voice and in his most famous work, *The Spirit of the Age* (1825), he can both laud and condemn an author in a single paragraph. His prose bristles with passion and enthusiasm. Scott's novels are 'like the betrothed of our hearts, bone of our bone, and flesh of our flesh, and we are jealous that anyone should be as much delighted or as thoroughly acquainted with their beauties as ourselves' (xi, 59) – which is sort of a playfully inverted-Kantian position, bearing in mind the German's imperative to demand the universal agreement of everyone else when you find something beautiful. But, having so passionately applauded the novels, Hazlitt rounds on Scott himself for self-deluding nostalgia and reactionary politics. Hazlitt cries out for quotation. He is one of the great essayists and an exemplary partisan critic, one who splices aesthetic values with political commitment in a way that could instruct some of the earnest politicized academics of today, with their pursed-lip disdain for literary delight.

One of the legacies of the Romantics, and the German idealist philosophy on which they drew, was the idea that literature mattered. Hazlitt's notion of the imagination was somewhat different from that of Coleridge and Wordsworth. It not only served a visionary, intensely subjective function, but also brought people together in shared experience. His *Table Talk* (1821–22) is a series on the ability of literature to humanize and dignify the business of living in the ordinary world. As the nineteenth century progressed, the value pendulum swung away from the isolated and elevated self of the Romantics and towards the contribution of art to society.

John Ruskin (1819–1900), the pre-eminent British art critic of the mid-nineteenth century, was greatly influenced by the Romantics but moved their aesthetic ideals towards more social concerns. The striving of the Romantic artist was a matter of *moral* strength and writers needed to curtail metaphors that distorted truth for simply poetic ends. He coined the term 'pathetic fallacy' to indict the ascription to nature of human emotions in order to achieve a certain poetic effect. Ruskin advocated the *integrity* in art, the importance of 'truth-to-life' and this, significantly, was a moral imperative. It was common to defend the arts in the eighteenth century for inculcating morality, or to regard aesthetic sensibility as akin to moral awareness, but it was Ruskin who saw the aesthetic purpose as itself moral.

If the Romantics were the first to present a coherent and sustained defence of the value of art, aside from its instrumental uses in moral instruction or social improvement, then Matthew Arnold (1822–88) could claim to have done something similar for criticism. He argues for a value for criticism prior to the arts, not just as handmaiden to them. In 'The Function of Criticism at the Present Time' (1864) he asserts, against the Romantic sanctification of creative originality, the dependence of art on the criticism surrounding it. Creative genius is not self-sustaining – it flourishes only in certain conditions and amongst these is the currency of ideas generated by a healthy critical culture. The intellectual atmosphere is not in the control of the creative power, but of the critical power. And only when the intellectual atmosphere is alive with a rich critical philosophy can the arts properly thrive.

Good criticism, for Arnold, echoing a Kantian conception about the aesthetic, is fundamentally based on *disinterestedness*. Its business is 'simply to know the best that is known and thought in the world, and by in its turn making this known, to create a current of true and fresh ideas' (*Essays in Criticism*, 18). This idea that the 'best' can be separated from the social context which mediates and legitimizes such value judgements, as if 'high' culture was separable from the context which produced it, is one that has left Arnold the whipping boy of great swathes of political critics in the present era. The idea of 'disinterestedness' is much resented by modern theorists, for whom the inevitable delusion of purportedly objective evaluation is seemingly summed up by callow understandings of this word. But much of what Arnold says seems to pose renewed challenges in the current climate. Though of course he shares many of the prejudices of his age, it is wrong to cast him, simply, as a mandarin or a snob, using culture to galvanize political authority. True culture, he insists, 'does not try to reach down to the level of inferior classes' but rather 'seeks to do away with classes; to make the best that has been thought and known in the world current everywhere; to make all men live in an atmosphere of sweetness and light, where they may use ideas, as it uses them itself, freely, – nourished and not bound by them' (*Culture and Anarchy*, 70). Moreover, his elevation of criticism as essential to the effective creation of art and poetry implies that the cloistered artwork should be set free into the wider circulation of ideas.

If Kant claimed art is disinterested, Arnold is advocating the recognition of this in critical practice. The critic should not measure the value of art against utilitarian yardsticks, whether they be Platonic ideas of ideal truth or the true tenets of the classics or the Protestant ideas of virtue. A healthy critical and intellectual culture avoids appealing to 'ulterior, political, practical considerations about ideas', but rather should strive to see 'the object as in itself it really is'.

But disinterestedness is not the same as an art-for-art's-sake separation from the 'real world'. Paradoxically, it is the very autonomy and impartiality of art and criticism that gives them a serious social role for Arnold. He was the first critic for whom criticism served an essential social need. Seeing his society in a state of dangerous disorder, with religion under grave scientific challenge, Arnold looked to culture not only as the mainstay of civilization but also as the force to fill the breach left in religion's absence. Religion, it seemed to Arnold, had been disabled by materialism, but the emotional and spiritual needs that religion had previously attended could find a haven in the arts.

The masterpieces of art and literature could sustain spiritual life. Criticism had a crucial role to play in the new surrogacy. Critics need to be disinterested, free from partisan politics, in order that they can create 'a current of true and fresh ideas'. In this way the critic prepares the way for the poet. In other words, Arnold inverts the old idea that criticism is parasitical on the arts. In-so-far as criticism creates the intellectual culture in which art flourishes, it is criticism, not creativity that comes first.

Arnold's pedagogical example was enduringly influential. Up until the postmodern scepticism about cultural value, it was a given that one of the purposes of English literary studies was to teach students the 'best' that had been thought or said in the world. There may have been some dispute about where the best was to be found, Eliot and Leavis may have wanted to re-jig the canon somewhat, but the idea of objective or disinterested aesthetic value marked the study of the arts until the late 1960s.

Arnold deployed the quasi-religious associations of the imagination for social and moral purposes. Art had a clear function within society, especially after the scientific challenges to religion. It was an antidote to a mechanistic and materialistic world, a source of spiritual sustenance and a balm for the disenchantments of modernity. In this respect, one could say that the value of the arts was as a generator of values. It operated to keep society together, to inculcate moral awareness.

In the late nineteenth century, a new attitude emerged which became known as the 'aesthetic movement'. Its founding father was the Oxford don Walter Pater (1839–94), who developed a cult of beauty that inspired a generation. In his essays and in his *Studies in the History of the Renaissance* (1873), Pater developed his credo that beauty was an end in itself that should be embraced for all its sensual, intense and life-enhancing pleasure. Earlier Victorian ideas of art, such as those espoused by Ruskin and Arnold, smacked too much of the functional and utilitarian. Giving art a moral and social purpose was to fly in the face of its special, non-instrumental status, like using a priceless antique display set for pouring the tea. The catch-cry of this movement became 'art for art's sake'. Art did not have a didactic purpose. It need only be beautiful. As Oscar Wilde (1854–1900), the most prominent aesthete of all, concluded his aphoristic 'Preface' to his novel *The Picture of Dorian Gray* (1891), 'All art is quite useless' (236).

For Pater, the point of art is the intensity of experience is provides, not its social, moral or religious good. His view of criticism, therefore, is not about programmatic application of rules or theories. It is about allowing the shimmering particularity of the art object to shine through:

> Many attempts have been made by writers on art and poetry to define beauty in the abstract, to express it in general terms, to find a universal formula for it. The value of such attempts has most often been in the suggestive and penetrating things said by the way. Such discussions help us little to enjoy what has been well done in art or poetry, to discriminate between what is more and what is less excellent in them, or to use words like beauty, excellence, art, poetry with more meaning than they would otherwise have. Beauty, like all other qualities presented to human experience, is relative; and the definition of it becomes unmeaning and useless in proportion to its abstract-ness. To define beauty, not in the most abstract, but in the

most concrete terms possible, to find, not a universal formula for it, but the formula, which expresses most adequately this or that special manifestation of it, is the aim of the true student of aesthetics. (xix)

The only way that the 'special manifestation' of beauty will be brought to light critically is through fateful articulation of an inevitably personal, subjective appreciation:

What is this song or picture, this engaging personality presented in life or in a book to *me*? What effect does it really produce on me? Does it give me pleasure? And, if so, what sort or degree of pleasure? How is my nature modified by its presence, and under its influence? The answer to these questions are the original facts with which the aesthetic critic has to do. (xix–xx)

So Pater's emphasis on beauty leads to a radical aesthetic individualism. He distinguishes his position from simple impressionism, where one person's experience of inferior art is equal to another's of a masterpiece, through a strong emphasis on discrimination. Though he avoids the 'universal formula', he is uncompromising about excellence and artistic quality.

Pater's *Renaissance* created a scandal. Its embrace of sensuousness and individualism is even more explicit in its notorious conclusion. What matters is not morality or religion, but the intensity and the ecstasy of experience. Pater advises us to grasp 'at any exquisite passion, or any contribution to knowledge that seems by a lifted horizon to set the spirit free for a moment, or any stirring of the senses, strange dyes, strange colours, and curious odours, or work of the artist's hands, or the face of one's friend' (189).

It was a doctrine that the young Oscar Wilde would find irresistible. He expands Pateresque individualism into a new and audacious theory of art and criticism. Some claim that Wilde's critical essays in *Intentions* (1891) anticipate the postmodern emphasis on the constitutive powers of language and human perception. The only reality we know is the one we perceive. But our perceptions come from a perspective which is heavily mediated and constructed by the culture in which we live. When you look at a sunset or a waterfall or a rat or an eagle, you observe them not as a neutral observer, but with all the associations and accretions that cleave to these things in our culture. The associations are generated by their presentation in a thousand stories, pictures and parables. 'For what is Nature? Nature is no great mother who has borne us. She is our creation. It is in our brain that she quickens to life. Things are because we see them, and what we see, and how we see it depends on the Arts that have influenced us' (312). In this way, for Wilde, it is not art that imitates life, but life that imitates art. As Vivian puts it in the aesthetic dialogue 'The Decay of Lying' (1889) 'Where, if not from the Impressionists, do we get those wonderful brown fogs that come creeping down our streets, blurring the gas-lamps and changing the houses into monstrous shadows?' (312).

For Wilde, culture and the arts redeem and uplift the banality and uniformity of the natural world. If art finds beauty in nature it is art that has put it there. Pater had claimed that the only way we can know art is by bearing individual witness to it. He had developed Arnold's assertion that the aim of a critic is to 'see the object as itself it really is' by giving it a subjective gloss – 'the first step towards seeing one's object as it really is, is to know one's own impression as it really is to discriminate it (xix). Wilde asserted that one's individual witness, be it the artist witnessing life or the critic witnessing the artwork, is inevitably a projection and an imposition or, to put it his way, 'a lie'. But, crucially, it is all the better for that. It is not representation but transformation that is elevating and redemptive about art and criticism.

So we have come full circle. Wilde accepts the Platonic idea that art is a distortion, but inverts Plato's evaluative distinction between original and copy. If art is 'a veil rather than a mirror', that is all to the good. Similarly criticism is a veil around art, it imposes its own glorious lies. The hierarchical relationship with 'life' on top, 'art' second, and criticism a poor Cinderella is radically destabilized and dismantled in Wilde's witty, aphoristic essays.

CHAPTER THREE

Science and Sensibility

Isn't there a basic antagonism between the very nature of a university and the very spirit of literature? The academic mind is cautious, tightly organised, fault-finding, competitive – and above all aware of other academic minds. Think of the atmosphere of suspicion implied by the habit of fitting out the most trivial quotation with a reference, as though it were applying for a job. (Gross, 315)

I

Authority shifted in the early twentieth century as the discipline of English started to gain respectability as an academic subject. Criticism went to university. The difficulty of grounding literary and artistic value, of finding standards against which it could be tested and measured, became ever more urgent. The new discipline needed measurable criteria. It could not examine students, or hold its head high beside the scientists at high table, if all it had to go on was a Pateresque notion of intensity of experience. In this context, critical judgements needed more than individual impressions for support. The dilemma that Hume faced – how do we reconcile the demands for criteria of taste and judgement with the diversities and idiosyncrasies of individual response – continued to trouble those who wanted to put criticism on a firm footing. But in the universities the question was not just a technical point of aesthetics. It was a question of professional repute.

That science could so clearly deliver the accumulative acquisition of knowledge, with such dramatically verifiable results in industry, technology and medicine, often made the 'softer' disciplines of the humanities uneasy and intimidated. The more ineffable 'truths' of art and philosophy would, in the twentieth century, often seek sanctuary behind the proven facts of science. Without a demonstrable proof for their decisions on what artworks were good and bad, some critics feared that, like cartoon characters who have just run off a cliff, they might look down and see nothing supporting them.

This anxiety is often present in twentieth-century academic criticism, with its ever-accumulating armoury of -ologies and -isms. Formalism, practical criticism, new criticism, psychoanalytic criticism, myth criticism, structuralism, semiotics, new historicism, genetic criticism: for all their differences, each of these movements seeks, in its own way, a quasi-scientific rigour. Such rigour has been variously found in the disciplined austerity of close textual scrutiny, the controlling categories of genre, the systematic procedures of psychology, sociology and political theory, or in the empirical and scholarly firmness of archival research. The very word 'research', which does service for all the various modes of academic literary enquiry, carries with it the impression of 'knowledge acquisition' that literary studies sought. Long before the hostility towards evaluative criticism shown by High Theory in the 1970s and 1980s, academic criticism eschewed the intuitive appeals to subjective appreciation upon which the nineteenth-century man-of-letters relied.

Yet there was an incipient contradiction here. Even as the academic critics imitated the techniques of science, its rigorous procedures and its valorisation of impartiality, there was a strong strand that continued the tradition of asserting the value of culture precisely as an antidote to the coldness of urban industrial society. The value of literature and the arts was, for many, to be found in its inculcation of humane fellow-feeling and moral intelligence. It lay not in science but in sensibility. Figures like F. R. Leavis (1895–1978) in the United Kingdom and Lionel Trilling (1905–75) in the United States kept this Arnoldian spirit alive through their criticism of the novel. The anaemic and dehumanizing world of industry and commerce, with its wholly instrumental and utilitarian logic, showed that the human and moral qualities of art and literature needed robust defence.

English became a university discipline because of the seriousness vouchsafed for the arts by those, like Arnold, who sought to provide it with a role as a surrogate religion. Literary criticism gained a foothold in the universities because it has a religious or non-scientific purpose. But this notion of English would often conflict with the urge to find firm, quasi-scientific criteria upon which literary judgement could be based. In other words the value *of* the arts often pulled against the attempts to ground evaluation *in* the arts. This led to an abiding tension, even contradiction, between the evaluative givens of the discipline and scientific impartiality of its procedures. This contradiction exploded in the final decades of the twentieth century, when a critical revolution in the universities attacked the premises about value which earlier critics and theorists had sought to establish.

II

So as the study of literature grew in the universities in the early decades of the twentieth century, a distinction developed between the 'reviewer', who writes for magazines and newspapers, and the 'academic' who writes critical monographs and articles for learned journals. The two streams are more separated now than they have ever been. There still is a crossover, especially in that end of magazine reviewing closest to academic concerns: the *Times Literary Supplement*, the *New York Review of Books*, the *London Review of Books* and the *New Yorker*, to name some of the most prominent examples. And there are still figures who have forged careers in both fields – John Sutherland and John Mullan, to name two London examples. But the gap between Ivory Tower and Grub Street has grown much wider, paradoxically at the same time as undergraduate numbers have surged.

'Theory' is usually brought out as the main culprit at this point. Its in-house jargon and dry technical philosophy is allegedly inaccessible to the non-initiate. Hence academic criticism has been steered away from the wider literate public it once enjoyed. Perhaps a more fundamental, and much older, explanation is the long-standing academic unease at a critical practice based on personal pleasure and response. While journalists can appeal to the discernment or enthusiasm of their readers, without going into spirals of explication as to how these evaluations can be grounded or justified, academics have been busy looking for an objective set of principles and procedures.

But surely the two poles, even when distinct, have often been healthiest and most publicly vibrant when closest together. Having a public audience makes university-based criticism less liable to bloodless theorization, while proximity to the scrutiny of a professional university community prevents reviewing culture from becoming slack and impressionistic. Furthermore, when academic criticism flows beyond its university audience, the effect is often to raise the prestige of non-academic reviewing culture too. This mutually beneficial proximity has frequently occurred from the platform of small magazines that seek to burst beyond specialized readerships. The cause and effect here is probably circular. It is not coincidental that the era of prominent university-based critics in the 1950s was also a time when individual non-academic newspaper critics wielded great power over public taste. The verdicts of the 'star' reviewers like Cyril Connolly (1903–74) and Harold Hobson (1904–92) on the *Sunday Times* or Philip Toynbee (1916–81) and Kenneth Tynan (1927–80) on the *Observer* mattered more than those of any single reviewer today. At the same time in America, a figure like Edmund Wilson (1895–1972), America's pre-eminent man-of-letters, enjoyed his heyday. Wilson worked outside the university system and, in *Axel's Castle* (1931); wrote one of the most influential and acclaimed critical books about modernist poetry. It is hard to imagine a figure like Wilson today, operating outside academic institutions yet at the same time substantially influencing teaching and research within them. It is because criticism has both an objective and a subjective quality, flitting between principle and prejudice, that it is in the land between the poles of scholarship and journalism, that it has often proven most fruitful.

Closeness, however, can also create controversy and contradiction. F. R. Leavis was often caught in a dilemma between the rigours of scholarship and the blandishments of journalism. If he was to realize the serious moral and social function of criticism, he had to avoid confining his message to small, specialized coteries. But at the same time he could not transform criticism into what he saw as another flabby mode of mass media. Otherwise it would simply be putting on the gaudy garb of the merely popular entertainment that it was culture's role to uplift and transform. The in-house journal of the Leavisites, *Scrutiny*, targeted the cliquish reviewing practices of London newspapers precisely because of its own aspirations to a non-academic readership. A more arcane periodical need not have cared so much. The Leavisites needed to emphasize the social and communal dimension to literature but at the same time save it from frivolity and dilletantism. But the need to educate and the need to edify often pulled in different directions.

More obviously, though, it is easy to see why academics and journalists might have had fraught moments in their relationship. Academics would sometimes look covetously at the wide audiences of literary reviewers, while pretending to look down upon their populist amateurism. On the other side, while journalists might feel intimidated by the weight of learning and intellectual prestige of the professors and envy their freedom from the exigencies of deadlines and copy, they could console themselves by the tiny audiences and esoteric fields of ever-increasing academic speciality.

III

In addition to 'academics' and 'journalists' one could identify a third broad grouping within twentieth-century criticism: novelists, poets and dramatists who supplement their 'creative' work with critical writing. They have had a huge effect not just on the reception of individual works, but in espousing critical and aesthetic mores. In the first decades of the twentieth century the new experimentation and innovation in the arts that would become known as 'modernism' needed explicators and theorists. Authors and artists themselves wrote essays and manifestos implicitly or explicitly defending the new artistic credo and many of the major modernist writers – T. S. Eliot (1888–1965), Virginia Woolf (1882–1941), D. H. Lawrence (1885–1930), Ezra Pound (1885–1972) – were also active as critics and reviewers. The modernist ethos tended to blur distinctions between literary genres and hierarchies, so previously underrated or populist genres like drama and the novel accrued critical attention for the first time. By the final decades of the nineteenth century, the novel had become the dominant literary form, but unlike the epic or tragedy, it had not been given any serious methodological or formal scrutiny. The American novelist Henry James (1843–1915) stepped into this breach and, in the prefaces to his own novels together with his writing for the *Times Literary Supplement*, was the first major theorist of the novel.

However, to find the seeds that germinated in the modernist innovations of the early twentieth century one needs to go to the last years of the nineteenth. Arthur Symons's *The Symbolist Movement in Literature* (1899) brought recognition in England to the French Symbolist poets, Baudelaire, Verlaine and Mallarmé. Yeats and Eliot both acknowledge their life-changing debt to this book. A friend of Wilde and Yeats, and a disciple of Pater, Symons (1865–1945) is the figure who bridges the divide between the decadents and aesthetes of the 1890s and the modernist attempt to overhaul and rejuvenate poetry. Poets like T. S. Eliot, Ezra Pound and T. E. Hulme (1883–1917) waged war against Victorian sentimentality and espoused a taut, restrained, objective sort of verse, as hard as flint and miles away from the narrative, moralistic or emotional versification of the Edwardians. The critical equivalent of this aesthetic, which would orient academic literary criticism from the 1920s onwards, was based on muscular close-reading focused closely on the text itself, not on an author's biography or the impressions of the reader. This sort of criticism, known as practical criticism in the UK and New Criticism in the USA, would become a way of fitting in with the prevailing literary values of literary modernism and at the same time answering the disciplinary need for rigour and procedural clarity.

After the decadent *fin-de-siècle*, literary culture took a bracing cold shower. The new social and political conditions and the cultural crisis brought on by the First World War made the calls for reinvention and renovation irresistible to a certain brand of high-brow literary intellectual. But this modernist project, following as it did Ezra Pound's famous motto 'Make it New', at a deeper level sought to make it old. Innovation and experiment in poetic form was undertaken to reconnect with lost cultural values and classical precepts. The figure who exerted the greatest influence in the first half of the twentieth century in his poetry and his criticism was T. S. Eliot. Like Hulme, Eliot's allegiance was to classicism, tradition, order and conservative values (the latter especially as he got older). Against the Romantic ethos of self-expression and revolt, he sought a return to authority and tradition. What mandates literary creativity is not the individuality of those who are living but rather a compact with the imaginative masterpieces of the dead. Originality of expression, the difficult, unfamiliar poetry that Eliot wrote, was not for the sake of novelty or idiosyncrasy but rather to be more properly, more faithfully traditional.

In 'Tradition and the Individual Talent' (1919) Eliot argues that artistic creativity is to be discovered not in any notion of individuality but in how far the poet accesses or brings to realization the 'tradition' – the living organic whole of Great Literature. Each artist writes as part of a tradition, 'not merely with his own generation in his bones, but with a feeling that the whole of the literature of Europe from Homer and within it the whole of the literature of his own country has a simultaneous existence and composes a simultaneous order' (41). Joining this tradition, then, is not simply a matter of imitating past literature: it is uncovering radically new forms appropriate to a new context. Through a completely new medium, such as Eliot's masterpiece *The Waste Land* (1922), written in collaboration with Pound, the past is articulated in the present and vice versa. In this way, an avant-garde poetic form moulds with a conservative politics, the new and disruptive put to the service of the old and organic. This prestigious club that makes up the Great Literary Tradition may every now and then admit a new member. But the underlying order and continuity is only strengthened by the introduction of the seemingly mould-breaking or disruptive.

To participate in this august process, to develop the true 'historic sense' as Eliot calls it, private psychology is forfeit to the wider organic order. The poet must revoke or transcend the individual self: 'Poetry is not a turning loose of emotion, but an escape from emotion; it is not the expression of personality, but an escape from personality' (48–9). Literary value does not have some universal basis in a timeless or idealized aesthetic, outside history, but it certainly does not reside in anything as impertinent as the eye-of-the beholder. Artistic values emerge through the long gestation of stable, orderly civilization. Critical judgement therefore gains its authority not through scientific principle but by working out a cultivated entente with precedence. This is how Eliot overcomes the troubling impressionistic or personal dimension of artistic appreciation: through the objectivity and authority of the literary past. Sensibility is about obtaining communion with this past through careful immersion in it and through abnegating the personality.

On the other hand, there can be no skeleton keys for the critic to unlock literary value either. An elaborate, a priori theory of criticism would be at once too bloodlessly abstract and too democratically accessible for a poetic ethos so steeped in history and hierarchy. There needs to be a certain mystery about obtaining the historical sense: 'there is no method except to be very intelligent' (9), as Eliot famously puts it in 'The Perfect Critic' (1920). But this certainly does not mean that he was content to let the individual 'intelligence' do all the critical work. Eliot wanted literature and literary criticism to be properly framed, girded, supported and stiffened. He achieved this by pruning back the object of concern. In the Preface to the 1928 edition of *The Sacred Wood*, Eliot writes 'when we are considering poetry we must consider it primarily as poetry and not another thing' (x). In other words it is *not* a document of an historical period or an expression of the author's intention. Still less is it a self-help tool for readers to bring their own subjective experiences to bear. It is a collection of independent artefacts and icons, separate from the mess of circumstance in composition or reception.

Such ideas would be the very vertebrae of a burgeoning academic criticism in disciplinary need of a backbone. Eliot does not put himself forward as a systematic critic, but the notion of an impersonal tradition and an ideologically neutral canon, the unified poem as verbal icon, the idea that a text has a unique realization pointing to one right reading – all had a huge impact on critical environment in the UK and America for the middle decades of the twentieth century.

   Nevertheless, as the critical tempo swung decisively leftward since the late 1960s, there has not surprisingly been a thorough reaction against Eliot's authoritarian style, hierarchical politics and exclusivist aesthetic ethos. His supposedly objective principles are, it is argued, clearly political prejudices. He talks of 'tradition' as if it were the most unquestionable and rooted thing in the world, eschewing the wholesale identification between it and the dominant culture. The 'European mind' is expressed mainly by the white, male, privileged classes. There might be some tinkering around with the invitation list, with Milton and the Romantics struck off, Donne, the Metaphysicals and the Jacobean dramatists included, but the Eliot canon is about as fixed, exclusive and hierarchical a literary guest-list as one could imagine. The drawbridge is very rarely lowered in this citadel. There is little room in Eliot for the recent concern with marginalized or repressed voices, for sub-traditions and counter-traditions. Nor, with the supposed banishment of personality, does Eliot ever recognize that his own prejudices might have dictated the canon he espouses. Under-girded though it claims to be by historical precedence (in the form of the 'tradition'), it is an extraordinarily hidebound, inflexible, untroubled sort of history. Eliot's insistence on the 'simultaneity' of the past in the present erases the notion that the past might be another country, that it might be frightening or culturally alien. Difference and plurality of outlook are eschewed in Eliot's search for authority.

   His intelligence is too subtle and his tone too restrained for his criticism to be dismissed simply as dyspeptic right-wing ranting. He gives the impression of intense consideration without ever seeming hesitant. However, while the importance of his poetry is unimpeachable, one can see why the evaluation of Eliot as critic, rather than the critical evaluation of Eliot, has plummeted since the 1970s. At the same time Virginia Woolf's reputation has thrived. While some critics regard her as contaminated by the patriarchal elitism of the Bloomsbury Group with which she was associated, she is one of the few critics of her era whose appearance on campuses now is not simply to show how dubious political views can masquerade as neutral aesthetic judgements. The resurgent feminist movement has (with some dissenting voices) employed Woolf as a figure who enriches aesthetic formalism with political and gender-consciousness. *A Room of One's Own* (1929) has become a totemic text for modern feminism and feminist literary theory, while her essays 'Modern Fiction' (1925) and 'Mr. Bennett and Mrs. Brown' (1923) have been defining manifestos of modernist fiction.

Woolf's novels and her critical prose show an awareness of the situated, socially mediated position of literature, which complicate the deracinated, authoritarian critical principles of her friend T. S. Eliot. She adopts a position comparable to his impersonal aesthetic in her unfavourable judgements of didacticism or personal indignation, which in her view tampers with the 'integrity' of Charlotte Brontë's *Jane Eyre*, for instance (95). But elsewhere she can show a countervailing tendency that sees in the author's effacement from the work the paradoxical realization of his or her deepest self: 'we do not know Jane Austen and we do not know Shakespeare, and for that very reason Jane Austen pervades every word that she wrote, and so does Shakespeare' (88).

Ultimately, Woolf was aware that writing is a mode of self-expression that emerges from particular conditions. The emphasis is partly because she is writing as a modernist novelist, where point of view and psychological impression takes the place of the slice-of-life realism of the Victorians and Edwardians, but it is also and inescapably because she is writing as a woman. She cannot therefore mistake gender privilege for objectivity. Just as her fiction is often concerned with the position from which observations take place, rather than the thing observed, Woolf's gift as critic shows a strong sense of *perspective*. This is luminously manifest in the anecdotal and metaphorical style that her essays often adopt, weaving and braiding their delicate arguments through elliptical and compelling imagery. It is also, however, because of her awareness that art does not occur at any time and place but can be impeded or enabled by social position and gender hierarchy:

> What were the conditions in which women lived, I asked myself; for fiction, imaginative work that is, is not dropped like a pebble upon the ground, as science may be; fiction is like a spider's web, attached ever so lightly perhaps, but still attached to life at all four corners. Often the attachment is scarcely perceptible; Shakespeare's plays, for instance, seem to hang there complete by themselves. But when the web is pulled askew, hooked up at the edge, torn in the middle, one remembers that these webs are not spun in mid-air, by incorporeal creatures, but are the work of suffering human beings, and are attached to grossly material things, like health and money and the houses we live in. (53–4)

Woolf's spider's web differs from the hard-flinty icon of the imagist poets or the well-wrought urn of the New Critics. While not reducing art to the material conditions of its production, she does insist on its vital connection to the historical context, the 'grossly material things'. Her position as a woman in a largely male literary tradition, with all the cultural and economic marginalization that entails, may have made her less prone to statements from an imagined critical Olympus favoured by some of her male contemporaries.

Implicitly, for Woolf, criticism as well as literature needs to be distinguished from science. It emerges, like the art it describes from social conditions and particular perspectives. What makes Woolf's criticism so vivid is the deft weaves of language and metaphor, her critical *practice* rather than any elaborate theory. At its best, such as in her writings on Henry James or Jane Austen, it reveals that the art of criticism is itself imaginative work, a web not a pebble.

IV

The professors had different problems. A criticism answerable to standards of objectivity and verification, not simply an individual's likes and dislikes, was to become the elusive quest of the university discipline of 'English' from the 1920s onwards. When English was introduced as a subject in Oxford University in 1893, it was with a strong philological emphasis, studying Old English and the history of the language. This was one way to make sure that it was a suitably austere discipline, grounded as far as possible from a likes and dislikes school of criticism. This medicine, it was deemed, should not come with a spoonful of sugar.

Yet if philology could side-step the evaluative questions implicitly posed by study of modern literature, it could not solve or settle them. The aesthetic movement of the 1890s had elevated the higher pleasures of art and the *impressions* it made on the sensitive spectator or reader. There were many dons, such as the Oxford classical scholar Henry Nettleship (1839–93), who regarded literature as an unsuitably soft and

effeminate subject for academic study, not least because of
these frivolous and effeminate associations. A university
discipline, for Nettleship, needed to be based on hard,
scholarly principles such as those that informed 'classics',
the bulwark of education in the humanities at the time. But
there were others, such as George Saintsbury (1845–1933) and
Arthur Quiller-Couch (1863–1944) who adopted the subjective,
impressionistic tone and sought to communicate their own
literary enthusiasms without being detained for too long by
methodological self-scrutiny.

But this credo was not going to endure in a university
discipline eager to gain respectability, to become an academic
subject based on decent verifiable standards. Criticism in
universities set its teeth against personal response and sought,
instead, precisely to uncover the 'Rule in Criticism' that
Saintsbury reviled. As English grew, it came more strongly to
be seen as a subject in search of a discipline, in need of reliable
procedures, rigorous thinking and assessable results.

To this disciplinary unease one could trace the moment
when modern criticism began to develop a troubled relationship with evaluation. Happily for the new university subject,
the modernist movement's assaults on emotionalism helped to
provide the requisite disciplinary moorings. Just as modernist
poets like T. S. Eliot and Ezra Pound sought to toughen and
strengthen versification, to cut out the trivial, inessential,
merely decorative and adjectival, so the critical theory that
began to develop after the First World War, when English
really became entrenched as a university discipline, sought to
imbue it with some procedural and disciplinary muscle. The
artwork *itself* became the chief object of concern, not its
impact on the reader or its historical origins.

It is significant, perhaps, that two of the key figures in

English Studies between the Wars, I. A. Richards (1893–1979) and his student William Empson (1906–84), both came to literary studies from other, 'firmer' disciplines: philosophy/psychology and mathematics respectively. Like the modernists, Richards sought to repudiate the commercial modes of entertainment which he felt relied on stock responses. He takes from the Russian Formalists – a group of Russian theoreticians who sought to subject 'literary' qualities of literature to analysis – the idea that literature should brush against the grain, should locate us in the realm of the unfamiliar. 'Nearly all good poetry is disconcerting,' he claims (*Practical Criticism*, 254).

In two major works Richards seeks to ground his subject in a harder basis than mere personal impression. Using the insights of modern psychology, *Principles of Literary Criticism* (1924) attempts to pull the methods of criticism and the principles of literary value under the umbrella of the new science. Richards embarks on what will become a familiar mission in literary study during the twentieth century: to submit its foundational premises to searching analysis, to settle once and for all the principles on which the discipline should be based. He wants to spring-clean the subject, dispensing with those aspects that are not essential and properly addressing its premises. A bit of sustained methodological scrutiny will give the subject the grounding it needs:

> [T]he questions which the critic seeks to answer, intricate though they are, do not seem to be extraordinarily difficult. What gives the experience of reading a certain poem its value? How is this experience better than another? Why prefer this picture to that? In which ways should we listen to music so as to receive the most valuable moments? Why is one opinion about works of art not as good as another? These are the

fundamental questions which criticism is required to answer, together with such preliminary questions – What *is* a picture, a poem, a piece of music? How can experiences be compared? What is value? – as may be required in order to approach these questions. (*Principles*, 2)

The 'preliminary questions' are, presumably, even less 'extraordinarily difficult' than the main ones. Yet, since Richards wrote, artistic criticism and theory still ponders them afresh. 'What is Art?' is a question which is as likely to be posed now as in Richards' time and with much less assurance of a satisfactory answer. Even the basic questions he asks, which seem to him the merest prolegomena to the business of criticism, now seem riddled with the cultural presuppositions of his time. 'Why is one opinion *not* as good as another?' In an age of the blogosphere and the reading group, few would make Richards' assumption that this question should be posed in the negative. Richards was neither the first nor the last to attempt a systematic outline of what criticism was for and how it should proceed. But it seems the tighter one tries to grip the 'principles' of criticism and evaluation the surer they are to slip between the fingers.

What Richards comes up with to gauge the 'values' of art ends up, not surprisingly, being a index of his own cultural context rather than an enduring set of principles. In *Principles of Literary Criticism* he espouses a sort of aesthetic utilitarianism. The proper objects of moral behaviour, the nineteenth-century Utilitarians had argued, were to be found by pursuing the greatest happiness for the greatest number of people. Richards, who cites Jeremy Bentham approvingly, applies this sort of calculus to the quality of a work of art which, put briefly, is to be measured by the number of 'appetencies' (impulses or desires) it satisfies in the individual. The problem of value, then, is solved by the language of psychology, even biology – 'all is right here and now in the nervous system' (246). Effectively, Richards brings behaviour-ist science to literary studies. Literature is studied as a site of psychological operations and should be judged only in terms of raising or failing to raise a response in the reader.

Richards recognizes that, like all scientific discoveries, his might be superseded by new advances: 'It should be borne in mind that the knowledge which the men of AD 3000 will possess, if all goes well, may make our aesthetics, all our psychology, all out modern theory of value, look pitiful. Poor indeed would be the prospect is this were not so' (4). Poor indeed. What he did not realize was that the fundamental premises of applying scientific methodology to responses, and of trying to quantify the problem of value in these utilitarian terms, would come to look misconceived. It is not the distance that Richards travelled that looks 'pitiful', but the very journey he strove to take. He fatally underestimates how nebulous and various the responses he sought to quantify would be, how differently and unpredictably readers would react. The science of psychology would not give the uniform, measurable guide to literary quality that Richards sought.

In a later work, *Practical Criticism* (1929), Richards turns more to the methods of close-reading that would influence American New Criticism. Here he demonstrates himself the vicissitudes of response. He records an experiment in which he distributed a series of unidentified poems amongst his Cambridge students and asked them to provide an evaluation. The results are notorious. Time-honoured and celebrated poets were derided, while those with a mediocre reputation were elevated. Richards wrote about the experiment in terms of the unformed critical intelligence of the students and, in his characteristically clinical and categorical way, sought to list and identify their weaknesses. He was sufficiently a figure of his time to believe that 'sensibility' was something that could and should be cultivated. And this cultivation would occur only in one direction. Close attention to the protocols of reading and interpretation would ensure the 'correct' response. Properly edified minds would lead to uniform critical tastes.

Richards tries to answer the vagaries of literary response by taking criticism to the laboratory. But at the same time he is Arnoldian enough to regard art and high culture as the solution to the aridity of scientific, industrial society. While he wishes to stiffen the sinews of literary studies with a good dose of scientific rigour, he sees literature as a life-raft 'as we discover how far out of our depth the flood-tide of science is carrying us' (350–1). Like Leavis and Eliot, he regards artistic cultivation as an antidote to mass culture, slack responses and the cold mechanization of urban industrialism. The difference is that Richards tries to beat science at its own game, using psychoanalysis or the tightly controlled methods of practical criticism in order to give literature a firm academic footing. Here, as elsewhere, the hunger for validation and disciplinary impartiality does not elbow out ideas of cultural sensibility and the values of the arts. It is to sustain these ideas, to put them to properly equipped social use (another of the senses of 'practical' criticism), that empirical methods are deployed. Throughout the history of academic criticism the implicit or explicit calls on scientific authority to justify literary critical practices, while at the same time holding culture as the redemptive alternative to science, would generate a tension that could easily teeter into outright contradiction. All that needed to happen was for the value-free methods of literary criticism do double back and collide with its quasi-religious purposes.

Despite his emphasis on appetite and satisfaction, Richards played a major role in directing interpretation away from a psychological basis towards the notion of poems as detached, self-explanatory objects such as those he gave his students to evaluate. This emphasis on the poem as a text that should be studied in isolation from its context (without deferring to author or history) created an aura of solid empirical enquiry that would prove irresistible to later critical movements such as the American New Criticism. Richards' methods, at their best, encouraged close attention to layers of textual meaning, the marbled qualities of poetic language and its tendency to mean more than one thing at once.

More than any other, William Empson brilliantly demonstrated the rich possibilities of this approach. In 1930, then 24 years old, Empson wrote his first major critical work, *Seven Types of Ambiguity*, in which he systematized the workings of 'ambiguity' in English poetry. For Empson, unfolding the manifold meanings within a poem allowed us to have an improved sense of its capaciousness and beauty. He was a gifted mathematics student before turning to English (working with Richards in the final year of his degree). His ordered, taxonomical criticism, treating poetry as a rationally analysable use of language, perhaps reveals something of the mathematical training. But there are none of the compulsions of computation here. Empson's reading of poetry is, like the man himself, tolerant of the wayward and the idiosyncratic, allowing room for fugitive nuances and contradictory implications. But despite the embrace of the motley and various, Empson's criticism has a civilized yet colloquial tone and sets about its poetic readings with an air of cool analysis. It knows what it is about and, while it is judicious and evaluative, it avoids any vague portentousness. Poetry is subjected to ever more deft and nuanced extractions of meaning, light thrown on its inward and obscured subtleties, tensions and contradictions the better to reveal its prismatic variegations.

There is an affinity between Empson's close-readings and several of the literary concepts beloved of American New Criticism. Where Empson privileges ambiguity, Cleanth Brooks (1906–94) was to focus on 'paradox', Allen Tate (1899–1979) on 'tension' and Wayne Booth (1921–2005) on 'irony'. But it is a mistake to regard Empson as simply the British wing of the American movement. The differences are ultimately more telling than the similarities. To begin with, he had more time for the author's intention than the New Critics, not as the final verdict on meaning but rather as one consideration in a poem's multiple significations. More important, though, is the different evaluative ethos. The emphasis of New Criticism tended more towards resolution and harmony than Empson's differentiated taxonomy. New Criticism tended to espouse the text's organic integrity in which paradox and irony were deployed in order to create a poetic effect, producing apparent contradiction only in order to erase it through the poem's aesthetic reconciliations.

As John Crowe Ransom (1888–1974), the founding father of New Criticism, put it: the poem is 'like a democratic state, so to speak, which realizes the end of the state without sacrificing the personal character of its citizens' (54). Empson leaves us with a more perforated and open-ended text than this. Both Empson and the New Critics embraced a methodology based on textual *focus*. Where they differed was that while Empson's conclusions were analytical, the New Critics read things closely in the service of synthesis. While the New Critics favoured *ambivalence* at the service of ultimate unity, Empson advanced *ambiguity*. Empson's interests, then, would seem more in line with the contemporary hostility to totalities, absolutes, and organic wholes, be they political or poetic. With a recent two-volume biography published by Oxford University Press, it could be that Empson's brilliant and subtle testimony to the quirks and echoes of poetic meaning will once again find an appreciative audience.

There were cultural and ideological reasons for this different emphasis between Empson and the New Critics. Many of the latter came from the antebellum American South, and could be nostalgic for a stable, organic culture, seeing the best works of literature as providing a balance, a depth and a complex richness which would operate as a balm to the rampant industrialism of twentieth-century American cities. The parallel between this implicit ideology and the espousal of the culturally redemptive possibilities of literature that, since Arnold, occupied a significant strain of critical theory in the UK is obvious. Ransom was a poet (like many of the other major figures associated with New Criticism), a professor of Kenyon College, Ohio and founder of the *Kenyon Review*. In the first issue, he reveals the mid-century sense that criticism was entering a Golden Age: 'Now is the Age of Criticism. I need only cite: Eliot, Richards, Empson, Tate, Winters, Blackmur – a list of intensive critics the like of which has certainly not been furnished in literary history at any one time before' (81–2).

The central plank of New Criticism was focusing on the text-as-text, without befuddling the issue with any appeals to authorial intention (let alone biography), historical background, or reader response. The classic exposition of the New

Critical rebuttal of the author's intention and the reader's response are recorded in two essays by W. K. Wimsatt (1907–75) and M. C. Beardsley (1915–85), 'The Intentional Fallacy' (1946) and 'The Affective Fallacy' (1949). Like the modernist aesthetic criteria of a generation before, these critics emphasized the hard, concrete, impersonal text, decrying notions of sincerity, spontaneity or any Romantic inkling that the poem should be judged as an expression of the poet's feelings. The feelings of the reader were given no more quarter: any attempt to judge a poem by emotive effect was judged illegitimate. The early Richards had sought to solve the problem of individual response by bringing it under the aegis of behaviourist science; the New Critics, recognizing that emotional variation leads to slack, un-academic relativism, barred it from the subject of enquiry altogether.

The poem for the New Critics implicitly operates as a harmonious whole, its deep and subtle workings accomplishing the organic interconnections lacking in a fragmented, industrial society. But, in retrospect, we can discern a problem here. How could the poem simultaneously be separated from social forces, yet at the same time act as a quasi-spiritual salve against mechanization and urban alienation? How could poetry be at once inviolably autonomous and culturally regenerative? Once again the attempts to find a rigorous basis for literary enquiry by focusing on the hard and unshakeable text, stripping away the inessential, the vague, the speculative, the 'mere' background, leant on an obscured contradiction between the scientific methodology and the spiritual basis for literary criticism. The price of methodological rigour was to leave the 'values' vulnerable. This would become a point of attack for a later, sceptical generation of literary and cultural theorists, seeking to expose the 'unexamined assumptions' and obscured political conservatism upon which the New Criticism allegedly rested.

V

Before the theoretical revolution of the late 1960s took place, however, there was another influential attempt to resolve the contradiction in regarding art as a balm for modern alienation while at the same holding it up as a socially uncontaminated icon. 'Mythic Criticism' became the dominant mode of North American criticism in the late 1950s and 1960s, opening the way for the arrival of French structuralist theory (which also looked at underlying frames and structures around which stories are shaped).

The most famous and influential exponent was the Canadian critic and clergyman Northrop Frye (1912–91) whose best-known work, *Anatomy of Criticism*, appeared in 1957. Frye espoused a value-free, classificatory analysis of literary history in which individual works can be understood as part of a vast cyclical whole. He elaborated on categories and types, regarding, for instance, the 'comic', 'romantic', 'tragic' and 'ironic' literary modes as having a deep correspondence with the seasonal cycles of spring, summer, autumn and winter. Like the New Critics, he repudiates a mode of criticism that draws on history, biography, moral ideas or references to the 'real' world. If they sought to firm up literary study through scrupulous analysis of the text, Frye extended this formalist bias to the supposed rhythms and cycles of literary history itself. He shifted the emphasis from literary works as isolated icons to establishing a relationship between them across history that was itself textual and narrative, based in mythic archetypes. The contradiction of New Criticism –

that literature is a salve to modern alienation but is at the same time be to studied without context, both the cure of social ills and blissfully untouched by anything other than its own organic textures – found a temporary solution in myth criticism. Literature is no longer rootless, but is connected to deep rhythms within nature and civilization. But Frye's is a distinctly de-contextualized sort of rootedness, his concern with literary archetypes shorn of excessive connection to social and historical experience. Literary history is treated itself like a self-contained text, with its own ahistorical laws and patterns.

Frye is the major twentieth-century critic whose status has most dramatically declined. Attempting to identify supposed mythic substrata of literature is a deeply unfashionable enterprise in the current critical climate, which tends to keep an eye out for political history lurking behind literary myth, rather than vice versa. Nevertheless *Anatomy of Criticism* was one of the most esteemed academic works of criticism of its generation and Frye's gifts of synthesis and elucidation, particularly on the Romantic poets, should be applauded.

What makes this work fit the narrative here, however, is Frye's consideration on the proper role of the critic, especially his efforts to underpin literary studies with the authority of science. Like Richards' *Principles*, Frye's *Anatomy* argues passionately that criticism can be based on sound scientific principles, that it should be a systematic, progressive body of knowledge. Hence the biological overture of the word 'Anatomy':

> Everyone who has seriously studied literature knows that the mental process involved is as coherent and progressive as the study of science. A precisely similar training of the mind takes

place, and a similar sense of the unity of the subject is built up.
(10–11)

Within the pages of Frye's 'Polemical Introduction' we can
discern the death of the public critic, or the explicit attempt to
separate the newspaper reviewer from the academic. In order
to base academic literary criticism on sound, objective criteria,
Frye feels the needs to distinguish it from journalistic taste
which, while harmless if it knows its place, should not be
confused with the sort of systematic enterprise that he is
about. Sharing literary passions and subjective enthusiasms is
a perfectly fine way to while away an entertaining public talk
or a newspaper article, but it should not be confused with the
objective rigours of lucid scientific criticism, with its
classificatory systems, underlying patterns and ritualistic
cycles. Frye draws down a decisive curtain between this sort
of activity and those 'public critics' who make up the 'history
of taste' (Lamb, Hazlitt, Saint-Beuve). It is a distinction
between the science of description and the art of evaluation:
'The public critic tends to episodic forms like the lecture and
the familiar essay, and his work is not a science, but another
kind of literary art' (8).

This possibility of value judgements outside the critic's own
prejudices or preferences are dismissed as 'the donkey's carrot
of literary criticism'. They should be relegated to the 'history
of taste'. He sets his teeth against evaluative criticism as being
insufficiently academic. Frye therefore turns his guns on the
strenuous efforts at the canon formation, revaluation and
scrutineering, undertaken by Eliot or Leavis:

> ... all the literary chit-chat which makes the reputations of
> poets boom and crash in an imaginary stock-exchange. That
> wealthy investor, Mr Eliot, after dumping Milton on the

market, is now buying him again; Donne has probably reached his peak and will begin to taper off; Tennyson may be in for a slight flutter but the Shelley stocks are still bearish. This sort of thing cannot be part of any systematic study, for a systematic study can only progress: whatever dithers or vacillates or reacts is merely leisure-class gossip. The history of taste is not more a part of the *structure* of criticism than the Huxley–Wilberforce debate is part of the structure of biological science. (18)

Its is a deft bit of rhetoric and no doubt the stock-exchange metaphor was deliberately aimed to wound: not just by deploying images of the tawdry commercialism that Leavis and Eliot would have decried but also because T. S. Eliot worked in a bank for many years. Even though Frye's criticism has an awesome, quasi-Romantic reach in its attempt to articulate the underlying, elemental grammar of genre, it disallows, in its scramble for scientific credibility, literary value judgement. But there is a clear contradiction in downgrading value judgements: it too is a value judgement. Frye's renunciation is supposedly of particular questions of literary reputation. But the value of literature itself, or the infrequency of his departures from the conventional canon, do not seem to trouble him. He does not recognize, for instance, that his casual invocations of 'great' art and 'masterpieces' could also be charged with being unscientific, based on accumulations of prejudice and social conditioning.

As so often, the supposed disavowal of personal response is in the service of deeper, less acknowledged and examined value judgements. There is no escaping evaluation at some level. Favouring neutral or impartially descriptive procedures is itself a value judgement. Furthermore, in Frye's case, even if literature is studied impartiality, its perceived function in society is anything but neutral. It connects with those elemental structures and stories that transcend history and articulate what it is to be human at the deepest level. One of the reasons why Frye, like the other critics of his period, had wide public reach was because of the large claims he made for literature, claims which a later academic critics were to treat as sceptically as he himself treated local judgements and literary chit chat. This is one of the ways in which the death of the critic was implicit in the golden age that preceded it. 'A public that tries to do without criticism,' Frye declares, 'and asserts that it knows what it wants or likes, brutalizes the arts and loses its cultural memory' (4). Regardless of whether one agrees or disagrees with this warning, it is clearly shot through with value judgement. Frye's effort to sideline evaluative criticism, while at the same time insisting on the value of criticism, would come to seem like having his cake and eating it too.

The end or purpose of Frye's criticism was to use scientific means to reveal a mythic unity that was anterior to the chaos of contemporary history. Frye aspired to use literature to reveal humanist unities behind cultural differences. But the prevailing cultural winds changed in the following years in the direction of plurality and multiplicity, not least because of the political need to accommodate difference and diversity. Frye's advocacy of the unity of the subject and attempt to elucidate the mythic strata of literature was attacked as regressive, 'liberal humanist' ideology. Frye wanted to establish the value *of* literary criticism by removing value judgements *in* literary criticism. It was easy to take the attack one step further and take on the assumptions of literary value as a whole. For all Frye's undoubted achievements as a critic, he dealt a body blow to evaluative criticism which would not only help split academic criticism from higher journalistic criticism, but would also mandate the ensuing attacks on his own critical achievements.

VI

The effort to accrue scientific credentials is one strain in twentieth-century academic criticism. Another is the insistence on the moral importance of literature, the idea that its depictions of a social world, in articulating enriching human qualities and complex social interaction, can morally 'elevate' readers as well as edifying them. The moral and the scientific could often be uncomfortably spliced together – overriding the incipient contradiction between the culturally partisan and the scientifically neutral. This 'moral' purpose varied from providing a quasi-religious antidote to the aridity of a mechanized, post-industrial society to refining and cultivating the sensibility of readers, giving them not just good aesthetic taste but also sharper and more nuanced powers of ethical judgement.

Moral criticism has tended to fall mostly on the novel. The realist novel showed the operations of morality not in any abstract rootless way but as it was actualized in social life, with all the dilemmas, compromises and specifics this involved. For the likes of the American critic Lionel Trilling, the novel was a socially progressive force that mediated against dogmatism and fanaticism and that encouraged fellow-feeling and imaginative generosity. Trilling is amongst the most important American public critics of the twentieth century. The subtlety of his arguments, his eloquence of prose and the capacious range of his concerns made him highly successful as a 'public' critic in American during the 1950s. Opposed to didacticism in all its forms, he belongs to no critical 'School'. The job of the critic, as he expresses it in *The Liberal Imagination* (1950), is precisely to be open to the variousness and possibility of literature, not to shoehorn it into a preset moral or political agenda:

> The job of criticism would seem to be, then, to recall liberalism to its first essential imagination of variousness and possibility, which implies the awareness of complexity and difficulty. To the carrying out of the job of criticizing the liberal imagination, literature has a unique relevance, not merely because so much of modern literature has explicitly directed itself upon politics, but more importantly because literature is the human activity that takes the fullest and most precise account of variousness, possibility, complexity, and difficulty. (xii–xiii)

But he could take an independent stand. For instance he rated Henry James above Theodor Dreiser, despite the latter's attention to the urban poor and economic inequality. For Trilling, Dreiser's mode of social realism, with its pre-decided political position, could thwart and iron out the complex and textured layers of social relations. History has vindicated his preference. Later in his career, when the critical environment had shifted and liberal critics were practising the subtle way of reading that Trilling had advocated in 1950, Trilling's *Beyond Culture* (1965) warned of the opposite danger – an overly effete or rarefied criticism in which literature is dislocated from its social condition.

Trilling most assuredly asserts the value of literature, but he uses it to probe the state of culture as a whole. This refusal to recognize the borders of close-reading placed him at odds with the prevailing New Critical climate in the universities, but boosted his role as a public critic, a goad to orthodoxy of left and right. He was closely associated with *The Partisan Review,* the most influential forum outside universities in America during the 1940s and 1950s. This magazine was the in-house journal of the 'New York Intellectuals', including Trilling, Irving Howe (1920–93), Philip Rahv (1908–73), Leslie Fiedler (1917–2003) and Susan Sontag (1933–2004).

By far the most prominent moral champion of the novel in Britain during the twentieth century is F. R. Leavis. Like Richards and Empson, Leavis was based in Cambridge, though he had a notoriously fractious relationship with the institution. Like them, he practised the close-reading of texts, but also espoused a moral, non-conformist zeal that would transform the understanding and teaching of literature in universities and schools in Britain. Significantly, of all the figures we are considering, Leavis was least beholden to a scientific or pseudo-scientific authority and the most overtly Arnoldian. He regards high culture as the antidote to the philistinism of a mechanistic, industrial civilization and does not seek to deck it up in the garb of the enemy. He reviles the vacuity that 'technologico-Benthamite civilization is creating and establishing in this country' and had many run-ins with I. A. Richards (*English Literature*, 24). If other critics found an objective grounding for literary evaluation in science or pseudo-science, this was not a strategy that Leavis would allow himself. Instead, to gird up his judgements, he resorts to strength of conviction, heat of advocacy, and the rigorous selectivity of his literary critical favours.

If Frye wanted to bar evaluation from systematic literary criticism, Leavis insisted on the absolute centrality of judgement and discrimination. Emphatic judgements represent a strong and healthy deployment of the evaluative faculty, a cultural rearguard action in a society overrun with potboiler novels and formulaic movies. It is not just 'what' is chosen, the exercise of the faculty of discrimination becomes an end in itself, quite above its application to literature or the assessment of individual texts: 'Discrimination is life, indiscrimination is death.' It is as if making value judgements is precisely what distinguishes us from the cold pseudo-impartiality of scientific utilitarianism (significantly, the one Dickens novel that Leavis allowed into his 'great tradition' was *Hard Times*, with its indictment of utilitarian ideas).

However, while discrimination may be central, Leavis compensates for its dangerous proximity to subjective likes and dislikes by keeping it on the tightest possible rein. While he likes strong judgements, these judgements can certainly not be made willy-nilly. He refuses the certainty of science in literary criticism, but insists on the certainty of sensibility. Leavis may have spurned the attempt to prove his evaluative judgements, but nobody could accuse him of not having the courage of his convictions. This is not a club which brooks much disagreement. If one is sufficiently cultivated, one will share his discriminations. The result is the obsessive selection of one author over another, the construction of small and exclusive canons that fervidly exclude all but a few claimants. His most influential book, *The Great Tradition* (1948), grants admission only to Jane Austen, George Eliot, Henry James, Joseph Conrad and D. H. Lawrence.

Writers have a duty to maintain the health of a language. He emphasized preservation rather than experimentation and thought that language should connect with 'Life', the highest word of praise in Leavis's distinctive lexicon. His cause took on the character of a religious mission. He became surrounded by band of fervent disciples and founded a journal, *Scrutiny*, that would expound the Leavisite position. The non-conformist Leavisites stripped the altar, espousing only the most denuded of literary traditions. Literature was austerely about life-affirmation and moral cultivation, but there was not much room for pleasure, transgression or individual taste.

The point is that this sort of rigorous discrimination gives Leavis 'that sense of absoluteness which seems necessary to robust culture', without having to fix these absolutes in the cement of quasi-empirical verification. The stridency of expression provides a compensation for Leavis's uneasiness with evaluative grounding or scientific proof. Ostensibly, at least, he does not allow a set of pre-ordained criteria to orbit evaluative judgements, he rejects standards that come before the critical engagement. Evaluation, for him, is not to bring 'an array of fixed and definite criteria to the given work, every work that makes itself felt as a challenge evokes, or generates, in the critic a fresh realization of the grounds and nature of judgement' (*English Literature*, 50). However the wisdom and tact of this open-minded evaluative procedure was not always honoured by Leavis. He often did bring fixed criteria to the work, a search for health and cultural 'hygiene', for instance, that he found in the vitalism of D. H. Lawrence. The ostensible disavowal of critical principle did not mean he could escape his own critical prejudice.

At the same time as brooking no disagreement, however, and to Leavis's credit, he recognizes that cultural values are not grounded in verifiable data in the same way as scientific facts. But this recognition does not commit him to jettisoning all external criteria for judgement, of abandoning it to individual caprice:

> the literary critical judgment is the type of all judgments and valuations belonging to what in my unphilosophical way I've formed the habit of calling the 'third realm' – the collabora-

tively created human world, the realm of what is *neither* public in the sense belonging to science (it can't be weighed or tripped over or brought into the laboratory or pointed to) *nor* merely private and personal (consider the nature of a language, of the language we can't do without – and literature is a manifestation of language). (*Nor Shall my Sword*, 1972, 98)

Like, for instance, John Carey, Leavis places a firm barrier between the realms of art and science. But unlike Carey's relativistic alternative, Leavis recognizes the excluded middle, or 'third realm'. He finds it in the 'collaboratively created human world' where our values mature, mellow, germinate and flourish. While Carey wants to keep the arts out of scientific territory, scorning the impertinent aestheticians who seek to buttress inevitably personal evaluations with scientific criteria, Leavis wants to keep out trespassers coming in the other direction. This is why, in one of the most notorious debates of the era, the so-called 'two cultures' debate, he so robustly resists the novelist C. P. Snow's claims that science should be ranked alongside the arts as the fountainhead of civilized values. Snow, in a lecture of 1959, had deplored the ignorance of science shown by literary intellectuals, whom he dubbed 'Luddites' and whom he accused of wilfully sidelining the beauties of scientific progress. Snow wanted science to be ranked as a cultural achievement alongside the arts.

Leavis's scathing response drew rebukes from the likes of George Steiner (b. 1929) and Lionel Trilling for its rudeness. But behind the ad hominem attacks on Snow's status as a novelist, there were telling ideas about where value judgement comes from and distinctions between the provinces of science and art. Science may, as Snow proclaims, be valuable and beautiful. But it does not reveal these 'qualities' in the laboratory or through the microscope. Values are not empirical. This is not to say that they are random, but rather that they are nurtured and cultivated through the 'collaboratively created human world' or, as he puts it here, through the processes of 'human responsibility':

> Well, science is obviously of great importance to mankind; it's of great cultural importance. But to say that is to make a value-judgement – a human judgement of value. The criteria of judgements of value and importance are determined by a sense of human nature and human need, and can't be arrived at by science itself; they aren't, and can't be, a product of scientific method, or anything like it. They are an expression of human responsibility. (*Nor Shall my Sword*, 140)

So, the idea that value judgements are not natural, but rather cultural, a discovery repeatedly used as a stick to beat evaluative criticism in the last 30 years, is anticipated by Leavis. He sees values not as timeless, absolute or innate, but as gestating within the processes of human civilization, generated by culture as well as used to judge it.

He underestimates that received value judgements can be an expression of human irresponsibility as well as responsibility, that the criteria of literary judgement can be implicated in dubious ideologies and hierarchies, that they can make sectional interests seem like universal truths and so on. Later cultural theory will fully dismantle canons and traditions rather than striving to overhaul or reinvent them like Leavis or Eliot. But Leavis still stands as a hugely dominant figure for a large portion of the twentieth century, who has been reviled not least because he was so influential. 'They say I have persecution mania,' he remarked once, convinced that the London literary establishment was out to get him, 'comes of being persecuted, you know'.

The persecution continues to the present in that Leavis is still a figure to be knocked down on campuses for exemplifying the sort of apolitical espousal of 'great traditions' of literature and the moral power of the novel that cultural studies movements see as elitist, liberal humanist naivety. It is understandable and necessary that those who fell under Leavis's long shadow would react against him. And there is much to criticize in Leavis, not least the zealous insistence that certain lessons only emerged from a correct way of reading a limited number of authors. He could give as good as he got when it came to scorn and acrimony and sometimes the personal antipathy directed towards him was personally earned.

However, on the credit side of his ledger must be the tireless polemical energy he brought to the study of literature. By treating literary studies as so socially important he boosted the status of culture and the status of the critic, spilling the energies of academic criticism out into a much wider arena. He is one of the few academic critics who have bequeathed their name to an immediately recognizable outlook and view of literature. For the Leavisites, literature and culture mattered. And therefore so did literary criticism.

Not least of the reasons why Leavis and Trilling stood as the foremost public critics on either sides of the Atlantic was their belief in the power of literature within real social conditions. Of course these academic critics of the 1950s should be overhauled, rebuked, questioned and re-examined. However, it is an irony, and a pity, that the major mid-century critics should be simply ceded, by a scornful cultural studies in thrall to its own radicalism, to the political Right. After the Oedipal reaction against Leavis in the 1970s, it is surely now time to give him, and the other dominant critics of the era, balanced consideration and recognition. These critics are still paraded before each generation of university students as ideologically befuddled, or reactionary bogeymen. The students deserve better. Especially since, as we shall see, the revolution against the critical ethos of the 'golden age' of criticism between 1948 and 1968 was incubated by many of the precepts of that age. The priest nurtured the acolyte who would eventually destroy him.

CHAPTER FOUR

The Rise of 'Cultural Studies'

I

Since 1970, criticism within the universities seemed to steer a different path from the world of letters outside. Paradoxically, this separation occurred around the same time as university student numbers boomed and popular culture received sustained and serious academic attention: two factors which, one might have thought, would open valves between the spheres. Individual academics often wrote for newspapers and magazines. There are still cross-over journals and periodicals. But the golden age of the critic, of which John Crowe Ransom spoke, seemed to have passed.

As discussed in Chapter 1, a notable redistribution of critical authority has occurred, a movement which has a new and intriguing dimension now with the development of the blogosphere. A general democratization has taken root. But apart from this decline in the role of the literary expert, the public imagination seems strikingly immune to issues and debates gripping teaching and research agendas in the universities. For instance, the declaration of the 'Death of the Author' convulsed literary studies, yet it did not overly trouble the commercial boom in the genre of literary biography, which a remarkably successful niche publishing phenomenon in the 1990s.

This chapter strives to address why this division occurred. It looks in broad terms at some of the developments in literary theory. My argument focuses on the academic avoidance of evaluative criticism during this period and, relatedly but distinctly, the value *of* criticism. I will be focusing, mainly, on the development of that cross-disciplinary academic behemoth that came to be known as 'cultural studies'. But, first, I want to look at the impact of structuralism and post-structuralism which, in the work of French thinkers like Roland Barthes (1915–80), Michel Foucault (1926–84), Jacques Derrida (1930–2004), Julia Kristeva (b. 1941), and Jacques Lacan (1901–81) would seep like dye through disparate schools of academic literary criticism from the late 1960s, leaving its hue in psychoanalysis, Marxism, feminism, post-colonialism, new historicism.

Drawing on linguistics, anthropology and psychology, 'structuralism', as the name suggests, is less interested in the ostensible content or real-world references of a work of literature than in the skeleton that holds it together, its architectural plan. All artworks are a part of an elaborate network of 'signs', governed by rules and conventions that underlie all sign systems, most obviously language itself. Identifying and calibrating these systems, not unlocking the unique mysteries of artistic meaning, is the role of interpretation. So, for instance, one branch of structuralism, 'narratology', seeks to elucidate the building blocks of stories, breaking them down into their underlying shapes and patterns. The genre of Romance fiction might be rendered thus: girl-meets-boy, girl-loses-boy, girl-finds-boy-again. Rather than talking about themes, characters or moral messages, a structuralist will tend to sift through the contents of a story in order to uncover its underlying syntax, its 'exposition', 'complication', and 'dénouement'. To pick a simple example, the story of the Garden of Eden will not be considered by the structuralist in religious terms, nor for what it says about power, authority and gender, but rather as an interlinked series of movements: 'up' (God's creation of Adam and Eve) and 'down' (eating the forbidden fruit), 'in' (serpent entering garden) and 'out' (the expulsion of Adam and Eve). If he does not actually use maps and diagrams in this exercise, the narratologist nevertheless thinks about narrative diagrammatically, about shape above sense, manner above matter.

Effectively, structuralism attempts to apply the rules and procedures of linguistic analysis to any human activity that 'signifies', including literature. The remit amounts to the whole of human 'culture' in its broad sense, from the fashion catwalk to the religious ceremony, from the soap powder commercial to the cave painting. Structuralism was the first of many assaults on literature as separable from other uses of language and from other manifestations of human culture. Literature was no longer 'special', its aura and mystique were stripped bare, behind the supposedly eternal verities or oracular wisdom of Shakespeare was unaccommodated structure, the same poor, bare, forked animal that could be found behind the soap opera or pulp novel.

Routing, or evading, literary value would have grave consequences for the public critic. But at the time, those in generational conflict with authority, flushed with the spirit of 1968, celebrated this de-mystification of the arts. Talk of canons, great traditions or timeless beauty belonged to the older, fustier generation, like bowler hats or monocles. How refreshing to able to get past all that cloistered, quasi-religious chatter, with its defence of elite sensibility and its palpable disdain for popular culture and the modern world.

However, this Oedipal assault on the old order contained crucial continuities too. Part of the allure of structuralism was the removal of those wayward, unquantifiable 'hunches' from literary study, its associations with taste and personal preference. In this respect the structuralist revolution, for all its innovations, promised to deliver a long-elusive quarry: disciplinary rigour. The science of structuralism seemed far preferable to the more subjective procedures of New Criticism which, as Jonathan Culler (the most eloquent advocate of structuralism in English), put it, 'offers but a more thorough and perceptive version of what every reader does for himself' (viii). Criticism for the structuralist is not just about reading and appreciating. It is about analysing and classifying according to stable linguistic procedures. Least of all it is about communicating our enthusiasms or value judgements. We can have our individual proclivities, however bizarre, but they should be confined to the privacy of our own homes.

As we saw in the last chapter, the urge to gird up 'Eng Lit', to give it some scientific trappings, dates from the earliest years of the discipline. In that respect structuralist literary criticism, with its borrowings from a muscular 1950s social science, was another attempt to expunge from the discipline its vestiges of dilletantism. Philology, which studied the historical development of language, had sought to achieve this when English was first studied in the universities. But now the science of 'linguistics' took on the old role of philology, no longer studying the *history* of language but rather its 'synchronic' (as opposed to 'diachronic') structure: how the network of words produces meaning at a given cross-section of time.

Getting rid of the subjective dimension, and repudiating the elitist associations of canons, traditions and evaluative judgements, was, as I have suggested, a double-edged sword. Structuralism studied literature as a particular use of language but, importantly, not one to get particularly excited about. Making judgements on what is 'good' or 'bad' has nothing to do with structural analysis, no more than effusing over the ineffable beauty of tulips and orchids would be appropriate in a scholarly study of botany. Literary appreciation was irrelevant to structuralism which, like any science, made a virtue of the impartiality of its method and would as happily treat a children's nursery rhyme as *Paradise Lost*. Both could be dismantled into their underlying systems, shapes and structures, the fall of Jack down the Hill was no less momentous than that of Satan from Paradise. The content of the story is no more than the occasion for its structure: the point of the exercise is not about evaluation but about analysis. The structuralist does not show public displays of affection.

Regarding poems and novels as 'sign systems' that only gained meaning through pre-existing rules and conventions, also usurped the idea of the author or artist as the originator or source of authority over the work. All words are second-hand, all stories are borrowed stories. In 1968, in a piece symptomatic of the anti-authoritarianism and revolutionary spirit of that totemic year, Roland Barthes wrote his famous essay, 'The Death of the Author', which argued that the meaning of a text is not found in the author's intention. The text floats free from the hands of its creator, its continually proliferating meanings realized in the act of reading, not that of production. Just as no one can stake a personal claim to language, which is of its nature a shared system of signs, authors do not 'own' the novels or plays published under their names. Everyone brings their prior experiences, beliefs, values and assumptions to reading. You are free to interpret texts in whatever way you want, without worrying about what the author 'intended' the text to mean. As Barthes triumphantly concludes, 'The birth of the reader must be at the cost of the death of the Author' (148).

'The Death of the Author' indicates an important shift of emphasis between structuralism and post-structuralism. Post-structuralism and 'deconstruction' challenged the supposed stabilities and steadiness of linguistic systems, emphasizing instead the arbitrariness and contingency of language. Structuralism had started in the 1950s, in the disciplines of anthropology and linguistics, as a 'hard' and scientific discipline, but as it developed these pretensions were attacked and questioned, often by those, like Barthes, previously grouped within its ranks. Part of its vulnerability came precisely from its all-encompassing remit, its tendency to see all human practice as based around signifying structures. If all human culture is subject to structuralist procedures, then, surely, so is structuralism itself. It too is a human practice. Structuralism is a language or meta-language, a system of signs about signs. There is no position from which you can observe structure, without being implicated in structure: the systems which structuralism purported to delineate cannot be observed from any perspective anterior to language, no more than you can gaze directly at your own eyeball.

Post-structuralism would assert that there is no way to get out of or behind the system of language, to measure it against any prior or non-linguistic truth. Structuralism had pointed out that any word obtained its meaning from the wider sign system of which it formed a part. So, in a sense, words only take their meanings from absent words. If someone tells you she came 'third' in a race, it implicitly means 'not first' 'not second', 'not fourth' and so on. Words taken as a whole are a bit like this: they are not autonomous independent counters, but only nodes in a network, each one ultimately reliant on all the others. This is perhaps clearest in considering the way oppositions or 'binaries' work. The word 'light' only makes sense in relation to 'dark', the word 'hard' to 'soft', 'up' to 'down', 'male' to 'female' and so on. If one pole in these pairings were not there, the other one would not make any sense. Therefore words are not autonomous and independent. They rely for their meaning not only on what they signify but also, crucially, on that which they do not, just as 'hot' relies on 'cold'. Post-structuralism exploited this sort of dependence, in which 'presence' is haunted by 'absence', that which is asserted and clear always inflected with the trace of the 'Other'. There is no word free from other words, only complex systems of inter-dependence.

Post-structuralism, like the postmodern thought with which it is closely related, took a profoundly sceptical, relativist direction, seeking to challenge the very fundamentals of Western conceptuality and metaphysics. It argues that all 'truth' or 'knowledge' is a product of language, that we cannot know outside the structural horizons of our own linguistic systems or 'discourses'. The hallowed avenues to truth, nurtured in Western culture since the Enlightenment – Reason, argument, evidence, empirical observation – are deeply, inextricably caught up in linguistic constructions. The very fabric of human identity, or, to use the jargon, 'subjectivity', is linguistic. It is not just that we understand ourselves through language (a mode of thinking based on the false belief that we could ever stand outside or before language); subjectivity is fundamentally constituted by language. In other words, if structuralism sought to elevate textual study into a science, post-structuralism sought to turn science into textual study. There is no truth outside our own humanly created horizons, no avenue to knowledge that is not itself part of human culture.

The (post)structuralist insistence on language as a system of signs, rather than a vehicle for meaning, turned out to be as unattractive to the literate public as it was compelling for academics. Not least of the aversion came from 'theory's' perceived impenetrability and its heavy, jargon-infested vocabulary. It no longer purported to offer expert guidance for the public, written in a style that signals the critic's own love and care for language and literature. But, I would argue, it was not structuralism or postmodernism alone that killed off the critic, but rather their infiltration of a new movement and ethos, which did not just ignore but often set its teeth against the very notion of 'literary' or 'artistic' quality: Cultural Studies.

II

In recent years, those critics of the 1940s and 1950s who continued the Jamesian tradition of evaluating novels according to their moral sensibility have become deeply, sinfully, unfashionable. The effort to put literature to moral work is blithely unaware of the political implications, its supposedly universal moral values a Trojan horse for normalizing the dominance of middle-class, white, male perspectives.

Yet the relationship between morally inspired criticism of the 1940s and 1950s and the politically orientated criticism of the 1970s and 1980s is based on stronger continuities than this repudiation would suggest. There is a clear line from F. R.

Leavis to Raymond Williams (1921–88) to Terry Eagleton (b. 1943). Both approaches, after all, seek to bring literature towards an ethical 'ought', both see literary criticism as a serious business that strives to make the world a better place. The key difference is that Leavis and Trilling focus on moral sensibility while the later generation, and one can include in this neo-Marxists, feminists, and post-colonialists, emphasize political consciousness. The arts are no longer about moral or cultural elevation but are rather treated as systems of codes that the critic must unscramble to reveal power structures within society. Critics analyse the text not to challenge their own moral precepts but more often to reveal something about the 'ideology' (often pernicious) of the society that produced it. While Leavis sought to shine a critical light on the moral work *of* the text, the later emphasis seeks to do political work *with* the text. Ask not, they imply, what literature can do for us, ask rather what we can do for literature.

So, in a sense, and in an affiliation that neither side would relish, Leavis is the forefather of political criticism in Britain. By focusing on the moral, life-affirming qualities of art, he had created a culture whereby artistic values were *instrumental*, directed at purposes outside the artwork's own merits. Or its 'merits' were gauged by non-artistic criteria. Historicist scholars had, hitherto, sought a deeper understanding of culture by appealing to history and society. Academic critics during the 1970s and 1980s inverted this endpoint, striving to gain a deeper understanding of politics by mobilizing literature and the arts. Decades of dislocated New Criticism, which looked at literature in a radically de-contextualized way, meant that the recognition that literature was implicated in history opened a floodgate. New Criticism and the practical criticism associated with it so closely regarded the text that they underrated the importance of context. Now, the opposite movement was occurring – critics were so geared to politics they stopped noticing literature. Or rather they sought always to look through the text. Literature became a mask that needed to be stripped aside to see the covert operations of power and privilege lurking behind it.

The French philosopher, historian and cultural critic Michel Foucault is the figure whose influence perhaps more than anyone else, surged through the humanities during the 1980s and 1990s. He brought structuralist principles and techniques to bear on a strongly historical and Marxist analysis. Cultural objects generate meaning not on their own, but only within given 'discourses', the networks of language and ideas which connect the individual in society and to which representation and truth is confined. These 'regimes of truth' are wired by the powerful, in order to preserve their dominance and influence (1980, 131). Discourse is power and power is discourse. But within this massive capillary system the artefact or artwork, rather than being a dense congregation of meanings separable from society, which can then be subject to investigation, analysis and evaluation, is only one of many 'cultural practices'. Just as cultural studies tears down the distinction between 'high' and 'low' culture, the masterpiece and the populist entertainment, it also perforates the distinction between culture as creation of any sort and the day-to-day behaviour of people within society. In other words the creative sense of culture becomes subsumed by the anthropological sense. Writing a poem, going to the cinema or brushing your teeth are all part of the complex ways in which meaning is generated and all are subject to the scrutiny of the cultural study experts keen to delineate the sustaining 'discourses' informing social practice.

The Birmingham Centre for Contemporary Cultural Studies (BCCC), which was to be the forerunner of the cultural studies movement in Britain and America, was founded by Stuart Hall (b. 1932) and others in 1964. The intellectual bulwarks were the British Marxist critics Raymond Williams and Richard Hoggart (b. 1918), both saturated in Leavis's influence. But as it developed in England, under the stewardship of Hall, who succeeded Hoggart as director of the BCCS, it shook off its Leavisite concern with literature and became more avowedly sociological, philosophical and political. The cultural studies own culture was, unsurprisingly, overtly left-wing. If you called it political, it would counter that all discourse is political, including the supposedly neutral techniques of traditional literary criticism – it is just that conservative values do not identify themselves as such, preferring to cloak this prejudice under the guise of 'human nature' or 'aesthetic value'. Those who want culture for the privileged few are objectionable elitists, those who want to spread it round and cultivate society as a whole are illegitimately universalizing their own liberal humanist middle-class values.

Cultural studies departments or institutes developed all over the UK and America in the coming years, often adjacent to or within departments of English or the Arts. More important than its growth as a separate discipline, however, is the waves it sent out around the humanities, as a set of both ideas and emphases. Its own borders – around 'culture' – were, anyhow, pretty impossible to draw, a feature in which cultural studies devotees took much satisfaction. The study of literature and the arts was increasingly pulled into a wider political project that was disdainful of both formalism (isolating the artwork from its context) and belle-lettrism. It was motivated by a radical politics (the spirit of the 1968 student revolutionaries, and their intellectual inspirations, was not far away in the early years) and highly mistrustful of aesthetic judgement of all sorts. Artistic evaluations were mere exercises of taste, a dubious sort of frippery that was shot through with unacknowledged prejudice and elitism. Indeed, the idea of high culture that Arnold and Leavis held up as the salvation of civilization became, in the eyes of some commentators, the enemy. Writing in 1969, the academic radical Louis Kampf admits that the very word culture makes him 'gag'. Of New York's Lincoln Center, built in an area hitherto given over to low-income housing, he declares, 'Not a performance should go by without disruption. The fountains should be dried with calcium chloride, the statuary pissed on, the walls smeared with shit' (426). In a symptom of the changing ethos in the teaching of the humanities, not long after expressing these views Kampf was elected president of the Modern Language Association, the foremost professional body for academic literary criticism.

Not all the radical academics wanted to deface centres for the performing arts. But many took on board the sociologist Pierre Bourdieu's (1930–2002) argument about the relationship between cultural value and social position. In his much-esteemed work, *Distinction: A Social Critique of the Judgement of Taste*, published in 1979 and translated into English in 1984, Bourdieu illustrates, through surveys and statistics, how 'highbrow' culture, opera and literary novels for instance, correlates strongly with social class, while the tastes of the lower orders tends to gravitate towards the less traditionally esteemed pop music or pulp fiction. Seldom has a sociological survey been at once so influential and so predictable. It will surely shock no one to know that Chopin and Balzac have a more devoted following in the wealthier suburbs than in the Parisian sink estates. It does not, however, mean that claims for the 'quality' of these artists is a ruse to keep the lower orders looking and feeling inferior. But this is precisely the conclusion drawn from Bourdieu's statistics by a generation of cultural studies experts. Judgements of aesthetic taste, they claim, are inherently class-based, ideological, designed to prop up the political status quo.

Rather than emphasizing the 'literary' or high culture, what Matthew Arnold called the 'best that has been taught and said', cultural studies turns its attentions, like the structuralism that influences it, to 'everything that has been taught and said'. In other words, Western culture is not about the accumulated masterpieces of its galleries, museums and libraries, but rather about all the practices of everyday life, from gardening to Gameboys. Cultural studies solved the problem of value not by scienticising it, *à la* Richards, grounding it in the sacred mysteries of Tradition, *à la* Eliot, or positioning it in redemptive opposition to mass culture, *à la* Leavis. Rather, it drove a steamroller over hierarchies, flattening all into indifferent cultural practices. Cultural studies will pay as much attention to your i-Pod as to the music you are listening to on it, to the billboards advertising the film as much as the film itself. It sets its teeth firmly against new critical 'delusions' that the text is self-enclosed or autonomous. Meanings are produced, reinforced and circulated in social matrices: artefacts or artworks are simply the nodal points where codes and meanings proliferate.

Though it does not make aesthetic judgements, cultural studies is not 'value-free'. It is motivated by a strong political agenda – left-wing, radical, distrustful of power. It often strives to expose the interests and ideology lurking behind the purportedly benign operations of much culture. The concept of 'hegemony', developed by the Italian Marxist theorist Antonio Gramsci (1891–1937) for the dominant, often unconscious, values and ideologies that prop up a society's hierarchical order, has been central to cultural studies. Artefacts and artworks are prodded into confessing their role in establishing and reinforcing the received ideas. So, for instance, a cultural studies approach to a popular romance novel might claim that it reinforces sexist prejudices; a police detective television show might be analysed to show how the power and authority of the police and the deviancy of the criminal is normalized and maintained rather than understood in political or social terms. More nuanced cultural studies practitioners will detect ambivalence, pointing at moments of ideological resistance as well as compliance. But the criterion of evaluation remains largely political.

As these examples suggest, one approach of cultural studies tends to regard popular culture as the product of capitalism's ideological manipulation of the masses. It is not hard to see an obscured Leavisite disdain for populist inertia here: PlayStations and professional football allegedly keep audience appetites numbed and predictable, turning them into biddable consumers. Another strain, however, would want to distinguish authentic popular culture from this manufactured mass culture. By attending to folk music, oral story-telling or local customs, experiences traditionally excluded from traditional critical and academic attention can be recorded, demotic 'voices' finally heard, emerging from 'below' and full of vibrant unacknowledged energies. Sometimes we can, allegedly, discern active postures of resistance within these folk cultures, anti-hegemonic moments that free participants momentarily from their ascribed social position and status. The concept of 'carnivalesque' as understood in this politically positive sense is associated with the Russian thinker Mikhail Bakhtin (1895–1975), who enjoyed considerable posthumous influence in the humanities in the 1980s and 1990s. The carnival is welcomed as an emancipatory form, where the restrictions of allotted roles and hierarchies are gleefully thrown off. Peasants can dress up as kings and men as women. Ribaldry and riotousness are unleashed in a beneficially transgressive articulation of popular energies, destabilizing identities and dismantling hierarchies.

Breaking down boundaries is part of the processes of emancipation – nothing is sacred, all must be subject to critique and sceptical analysis. If carnivalesque artforms are preferred for their performance of scrambled identities, cultural studies also likes to puncture, subvert and adulterate. It deliberately sets out to rethink institutional classifications, or the rigidities of traditionally sequestered subjects, toppling the borders of 'literature', 'history', 'geography' and so forth. Cultural studies sets as its area of enquiry the whole of 'culture', understood in its broadest sense.

But there are dangers here. If 'culture' means all human practice then from what position can a boundary be drawn around it so that one can say something meaningful about it? How can we diagnose something that so irremediably implicates us? How can you ever get outside 'culture' in order to examine it with any degree of objectivity? Cultural studies, so eager to escape the institutional limitations of conventional disciplinary distinction, ends up being quite impenetrable, hard to fix or identify. It cannot be called to account because it refuses the account book. This might be one reason why it has been so hard to popularize. To be concerned with everything is, ultimately, to be concerned with nothing.

As an example of these dangers, and the ethos of cultural

studies generally, consider the editorial statement that the journal *Cultural Studies* (1987–), one of the leading academic journals in the field, sported in the mid-1990s:

> the journal seeks work that explores the relation between everyday life, cultural practices, and material, economic, political, geographical and historical contexts; that understands cultural studies as an analytic of social change; that addresses a widening range of topic areas, including post- and neo-colonial relations, the politics of popular culture, issues in nationality, transnationality and globalization, the performance of gendered, sexual and queer identities, and the organization of power around differences in race, class, ethnicity etc.; that reflects on the status of cultural studies; and that pursues the theoretical implications and underpinnings of practical inquiry and critique.

Is that all? It would surely have been easier to list what cultural studies is not about. Is there an area of human activity that is left out of a list that includes 'everyday life', 'cultural practices', the 'politics of popular culture', not to mention 'material, economic, political, geographical and historical contexts'? Just in case something is omitted, the intention to address a 'widening range of topics areas' is included in the manifesto, signalling, like any global corporation, or nascent empire, the intention to expand. The only unifying element in this broad reach of topics is the underlying *raison-d'être* for the enterprise, namely 'an analytic of social change'. The expansiveness of disciplinary reach is contrasted with a narrow, po-faced political agenda, expressed in the vaguest manner but ticking all the boxes of race, gender, class and colonialism. It relies on its academic audience to share its value system, to understand the shorthand of its pre-cooked political programme: the 'etc.' there is very telling. For all the routine disdain for aesthetic values, this branch of cultural studies is very upfront about its political ones.

In the contemporary study of the humanities in universities in the UK and the USA, being 'inter-disciplinary' is usually presented as an unalloyed good. Boasting that you are devoted to 'uni-disciplinary' research is unlikely to get you a tenured academic post. Inter- and multi-disciplinary work can often be mutually enriching, but the huge disciplinary range of cultural studies threatens to stretch it beyond its usefulness, mandating an encroachment into disciplinary areas where angels fear to tread. Not surprisingly the members of some disciplines, who felt that their claims to truth extended beyond social constructions, found the postmodern claims about their subject impertinent and ill-informed. A case in point is the notorious 'Sokal Hoax'. In the mid-1990s the academic journal *Social Text* accepted for publication an article by the New York University physicist Alan Sokal that purported to be a sociological critique of scientific method. The article deployed the vocabulary of postmodern theory to cast doubt over the truth-claims of science. It was, of course, a hoax designed to discredit the pretensions and dubious credentials of cultural studies. When the article was published, Sokal went public with the scandal, much to the delight of huge swathes of the popular press.

During the 1980s and 1990s there was a hipness to cultural studies amongst undergraduates, for whom cyborg theory or the semiotics of the fashion industry seemed a lot more glamorous than assessing nature imagery in Samuel Daniel's sonnets. But despite its massive influence in the universities, despite its much-celebrated violation of disciplinary and institutional boundaries, and despite its on-the-barricades anti-elitism, the attitudes and ethos of cultural studies were strikingly ineffective at reaching a wider public audience. One might have thought that when criticism started to pay attention to what the majority of people actually did during their leisure hours it would obtain a boost in popular interest. But the more cultural studies looked at discos and detective fiction, *Cosmopolitan* and car advertisements, it seemed the general public drifted further and further away from the sorts of criticism the universities were producing.

People were not turned off by popular culture itself. There is clearly a public appetite for critical discussion of mainstream entertainment, which is why serious newspapers and magazines have devoted increasing space to it. It was not the subject matter that alienated a wide audience, but the way it was treated: in dry sociological language and as a means to a political end. Invoking low culture was not to complicate or puncture the low–high distinction but rather to elbow out both. By contrast those critics who examined popular culture alert to its pleasures found the wider public more ready to listen to what they had to say. If Roland Barthes had more public penetration than other structuralist philosophers, it was partly because the pleasures of reading and seeing were at the centre of his work, and he wrote about them in an idiosyncratic, essayistic style that was itself stimulating and attractive.

Writing about the value and delights of art does not mean that a critic lacks ethical commitments or social engagement. Susan Sontag was an unapologetic aesthete whose literary and artistic judgements nonetheless bristled with political and social awareness. Public intellectual, novelist, playwright, essayist, and activist, Sontag wrote about drugs, cinema, photography, high literature, politics and theory. She was closely associated with the left-wing, anti-Stalinist New York periodical *Partisan Review*. In one of her most famous early essays, 'Against Interpretation' (1966), Sontag fires a broadside against the state of current criticism at the height of the structuralist vogue. She opposes the disintegrative momentum of literary interpretation with its separation of form and content and its division of the text into constituent themes and topics. Her article, which might be called 'Against Analysis', is disturbed by the violation that the scientific methods of interpretation have visited on art. 'In place of a hermeneutics we need an erotics of art', she provocatively declares (14). Against an academic theory that had sought to firm up the bases of academic criticism by turning it into a form of mechanics, Sontag defended the indivisible integrity of the artwork.

This influential essay was buttressed in the collection *Against Interpretation* (1966) by 'Notes on Camp' (originally her first *Partisan Review* publication in 1964). The idea of 'camp', now domesticated almost wholly into gay culture, was used in Sontag's hands as a key to popular cultural modes and the aesthetics of the modern. The politics of style are flamboyantly mobilized to displace and disrupt received identities in a sensibility that is politically liberating because it repudiates earnestness: 'Camp is the consistently aesthetic experience of the world. It incarnates a victory of "style" over "content," "aesthetics" over "morality," of irony over tragedy' (287). Written in a series of aphorisms, the essay aims for epigrammatic quotability: 'The whole point of Camp is to dethrone the serious. Camp is playful, anti-serious. More precisely, Camp involves a new, more complex relation to "the serious." One can be serious about the frivolous, frivolous about the serious' (288).

Later in her career, she expressed some misgivings about the direction of a culture all too quick to 'dethrone the serious' not for the subversive frivolity but for banal superficiality. But her espousals in these early essays are an antidote to the systematic emphasis of criticism as it had grown in the universities. Perhaps it required a public intellectual like Sontag, without a close university affiliation, to revive the Wildean outlook, rescuing the non-utilitarian, non-scientific qualities of art from the academics. As in the case of Wilde, the repudiation of 'instrumental' art was nonetheless in the service of a more profound politics. Sontag was moral without being moralistic, political without being didactic. She demonstrates that the best way, politically and aesthetically, to tackle cultural snobbery and exclusivity are not to repudiate artistic value but rather to appropriate it: 'The experiences of Camp are based on the great discovery that the sensibility of high culture has no monopoly upon refinement' (291).

The general attention to popular culture in the newspapers and magazines from the 1980s comes from figures like Sontag and Pauline Kael, not from the universities. It is not a journalistic outgrowth of cultural studies but rather the opposite impulse: applying to popular forms like film, television drama or genre fiction an evaluative and aesthetic treatment that academics usually disavow. It is the difference between elevating culture to the level of the aesthetic and reducing aesthetics to the level of the cultural.

In the hands of cultural studies all artforms, high and low, become flattened into systems of cultural signs. Cultural studies often overrides distinctions between creativity and any other form of social practice, between culture as 'making' and culture as 'doing', between production and consumption. Its sociological preoccupations mean that making a film or writing a book are no more intrinsically deserving of critique or analysis than going to the cinema or the reading group. 'Creativity', with its notions of individual agency or imagination, is one of the supposedly 'liberal humanist' concepts that cultural studies spurns, preferring instead the term 'construction' – a favoured word in the contemporary humanities. Sexual, racial, national identities and social roles are all 'constructed' or 'performed' within the prevailing culture. We should not consider individual artefacts, like novels or plays, as being created by any individual or even discrete group. The author or director is simply the cipher for social norms, attitudes, assumptions and ideologies and it is these that should be critiqued. The arts adopt a transparent, porous quality: they are there not to be looked at so much as looked through. This is one reason that cultural studies is so keen to go along with the 'Death of the Author' – the constraints of intentionality, finite meaning, responsibility, and creativity need to be sloughed off if the 'text' is going to be put to good political work.

The sense that some one person is responsible for an artwork, that the finished product has some determinate relationship with what an artist intended, tends to go hand in hand with artistic judgements of value. But notions of 'intention', let alone 'imagination', are regarded as antediluvian in certain academic circles. The more the artwork or novel or poem gets submerged into the flux of social signs around it, the more invisible it becomes. This is precisely the opposite error of those New Critics who insisted on disconnecting the text from its context. One can and should recognize the implication of art in society and history. But without also circumscribing and isolating it, treating it as having some determinate relationship with its creator, we cannot meaningfully evaluate it.

If criticism forsakes evaluation, it also loses its connections with a wider public. This is why it is cultural studies, more than any other academic phenomenon, that has led to the death of the critic. To command wide public attention, the critic needs to write as if the stakes matter, that the arts are important and the questions to be arbitrated and judged upon are ones of some moment – not just politically but also aesthetically (the two are interlaced). If we do not attend to value *in* the arts, then how can we attend to the value *of* the arts?

III

None of this is to suggest that the arts and literature should be kept away from politics, history and sociology. That would be the equivalent of saying that they have nothing to do with the real world. There is no returning to a criticism of well-wrought urns and timeless masterpieces uncontaminated by worldly associations. Art and literature are historical and, hence, political. But this does not mean that literature should merely be an outpost of politics, no more than – because political writings can be read as textual and literary – politics should be an outpost of English. Holding the arts to account only for their ideological and political position is the equivalent, in the sphere of criticism, to socialist realism, the officially approved type of art in the Soviet Union. Marxist intellectuals worth their salt have long repudiated that sort of vulgar 'girl-meets-tractor' drama, which is judged in so far as it toes the party line. But the earnest political emphasis of cultural studies, albeit broadened to include race, gender, sexual orientation and ethnicity, can seem narrowly focused, for all the profligate abundance of its subject matter. If socialist realism demanded that art addresses itself to political subjects, much modern theory demands the same of criticism. Neither art nor criticism needs the stricture.

The interface between art and politics, literature and society, need not be so reductive. Some may lament the direction that cultural studies took, but its origins in the work of Raymond Williams reveal how attractive and powerful the synergy between literature and politics could be. Williams deployed the Leavisite belief that literature had a serious moral and social purpose, but took it decisively leftwards, melding it with the Marxist ideas of Bertolt Brecht (1898–1956) and Georg Lukács (1885–1971). The idea that the salvation of society lay in high culture shifted to a much broader more inclusive, more politicized consideration of the interaction of culture and society. He rejected the Leavisite notion of a deleterious 'mass culture' majestically repudiating the whole concept of the 'masses' and the nefarious ideology which underpins it: 'There are in fact no masses; there are only ways of seeing people as masses' (289).

In *Culture and Society 1780–1850* (1958) and *The Long Revolution* (1961) Williams wrestled with the relationship between cultural texts and their contexts, at a time when that relationship had long been evaded or domesticated in academic literary criticism. Puncturing the disciplinary separations between literature, culture and politics, he insists that literature and language cannot be considered in any rootless or ahistorical space. He considers for instance the various definitions and techniques of literary 'realism' – social and personal, documentary and formula – as a means of representing and critiquing society. More importantly, perhaps, and more influential on the development of cultural studies, he extends his field of enquiry to entire systems of communication, attending to the formative power of education, literacy, television, film, the mass media and the popular press – the active social relationships that govern the transfer of cultural ideas.

Williams often probes and worries the contours of meaning within words and concepts, tracing the evolution of their significations and associations over time, reading them like runes in which can be deciphered the values and assumptions of different era. Social and cultural processes occur within language and by a sort of politicized etymology we can discern mutating cultural attitudes in words, like tracing the rings on a tree-stump. *Keywords* (1976), first developed as an appendix to *Culture and Society*, gives this archaeology of a select vocabulary of significant words and concepts : 'class', 'democracy', 'nature' ('perhaps the most complex word in the language'),'realism' 'society', 'subjective', 'work' and many more. Williams teases and feels out the multiple senses of these keywords, coaxing out their layers of meaning and ambiguity.

Williams's ideas nurtured the cultural studies that would, as I have been arguing, steer academic criticism away from a wide public audience. However, this did not happen with Williams himself, who exemplified more than any other figure of his era the politically committed public intellectual. He wrote prodigiously in many modes and registers. His academic writings are often condensed, gnarled and conceptually ambitious, but he was also active as a journalist, pamphleteer, polemicist, playwright and novelist. He wrote on television for *The Listener* and was a regular book reviewer in the *Guardian* and *New Society*. During the 1960s and 1970s, Williams was active in British left-wing politics, the Labour Party, the Campaign for Nuclear Disarmament and the anti-Vietnam movement. He was a decisive figure in the formation of the *New Left Review* (1960–), an intellectual journal of the left that bridges academic and high-journalistic arenas.

Williams was an inspirational figure for generations of left-wing academics. He is the one who, more than anyone, threw open the window of academic English studies, demonstrating the inexorable involvement of culture in the society which forms it. The most significant English-speaking Marxist literary critic of the twentieth century, he is a pioneer for all the politically motivated critical approaches, from feminism to post-colonialism to queer studies, that have dominated the humanities for the past 30 years.

Nevertheless, for all his achievements, Williams opened the door for the demystification of literary studies that, while initially boosting its social relevance, would eventually sever the work of the critic from public interest. In 1958, Williams wrote a well-known essay, 'Culture is Ordinary', a title that indicates both the attractions and the perils of the path he took. One can surely sympathize with his urge to democratize the arts, to appropriate them from the cloistered dons and the privileged toffs. Yet the problem with reacting against the elite position of the arts within society, of stripping their aura or puncturing their claims to special treatment, is that they thereby can cease to be distinct, precious, valuable. If the arts are so 'ordinary', why should the public – in whose name the arts are being reclaimed – be interested in them? Why should art or literature get more respect or attention than any other form of entertainment? Why, certainly, should the critic be given a privileged position as an authoritative commentator? John Gross was surely prophetic in 1969 when, in rightly predicting Williams's enduring role in academic criticism, he cast doubt on whether this influence would extend outside academic circles. 'When he affirms that culture is "ordinary", one may applaud his attempt to strip the word of its snobbish or daunting connotations, and yet feel impelled to add that in literature, at least, ordinariness is a very limited virtue' (319).

These early heady days of cultural studies were exhilarating in many ways: the arts, so long sequestered in literal and figurative museums, were ventilated by recognition of their location within history. Even more importantly, a figure like Williams spurns the so-called 'vulgar Marxist' idea that culture simply reflects prevailing interests. He considers it as a site where power is resisted as well as reinforced. Academic critics take on by implication a very serious role indeed. Rather than functioning as custodians for the arts, or protectors and occasional explicators of timeless masterpieces of civilization, they become cultural and political agents in their own right, active in the mobilization of culture in the cause of political consciousness. Flushed and heady with this sense of professional importance, you can easily see why younger academics in the 1970s would want to be part of this new movement. Why not exchange a dwindling revenue of cultural capital for the allure of political activism? No longer a parasitical pastime, the end of criticism is no longer the 'Work', but the work to which the Work can be put.

It is hard to overestimate just how overt the political agenda in the humanities has become in the last 30 years. The ethos of cultural studies, and the spirit of '68 which impelled it forward, has been unstoppable, fuelled by a sense of its own iconoclasm, its own radicalism. That the Left found a haven in the humanities in the last decades of the twentieth century may nonetheless be a symptom of socialism in retreat. The heyday of Theory was in the 1980s, as the Eastern Bloc teetered towards its collapse and the free-market ideologies gained ascendancy in the West. The failure of left-wing politics during the Thatcher and Reagan administrations left it unmoored with nowhere to go. Many of its intellectual energies were diverted into humanities departments, where it could unleash the most uncompromising radicalism against the very foundational philosophies of Western Civilization, without actually doing too much damage outside the seminar room. Referring to the deployment by cultural studies of postmodern and post-structuralist principles, Richard Rorty puts the case trenchantly:

> The contemporary academic Left seems to think that the higher your level of abstraction, the more subversive of the established order you can be. The more sweeping and novel your conceptual apparatus, the more radical your critique … These futile attempts to philosophize one's way into political relevance are a symptom of what happens when a Left retreats from activism and adopts a spectatorial approach to the problems of its country. Disengagement from practice produces theoretical hallucinations. (92–4)

Subjects like English, with its deep-rooted contradictions and long-standing methodological anxieties, seemed ripe for overhauling. The efforts to imbue the discipline with foundations and rigour, which had so exercised critics from Richards to Frye, were swept aside by a new impulse to inter- and multi-disciplinarity. In 'Eng Lit' courses the word 'text', sleek, cold and scientific, has taken over from those warm, value-laden words 'novel', 'poem' or 'play'. The term 'literature' itself has come in for sceptical debunking. It tends, for instance, to be held with forceps when treated in undergraduate theory primers. They routinely start off by exposing the ideological constructions of what we understand by the term.

One leading student guide, for instance, views with great distaste 'what has gone on in its sullied name, and under its tattered banner' (Saldan, 2).

Students then learn of the tainted, politically noxious and reactionary development of the discipline that they have chosen to study. A number of colluding factors made 'English' (and the nationalistic aura of the name is significant) perform its allegedly conservative work. When science began to undercut the traditional role of religion in society in the mid-Victorian period, English stepped into the ideological breach, espousing and reinforcing the values of the middle-classes, creating an aura of nationalist grandeur to reinforce and disseminate 'hegemony' abroad and at home during the height of British imperialism. It did so with the justification that it was above politics and history, concerned only with eternal verities about 'life'. The attitude is caustically summed up by Terry Eagleton:

> Since literature, as we know, deals in universal human values rather than in such historical trivia as civil wars, the oppression of women or the dispossession of the English peasantry, it could serve to place in cosmic perspective the petty demands of working people for decent living conditions or greater control over their own lives, and might even with luck come to render them oblivious to such issues in their high-minded contemplation of eternal truths and beauties. (*Introduction to Literary Theory*, 25)

Eagleton, a student of Williams in Cambridge, became the standard-bearer of Marxist criticism during the 1980s. His *Literary Theory: An Introduction* is one of the highest-selling undergraduate primers ever published and has had a massive impact on the way literature is taught and studied. It describes and explains the origin of the discipline of 'English' and goes through the various theoretical approaches of the twentieth century: formalism, New Criticism, hermeneutics, psychoanalysis, structuralism and post-structuralism. Eagleton's technique here, as in his other books on ideology and aesthetics, is to summarize a position in order to expose and unveil its underlying 'ideology', the partisan and political motivations that lurk behind even the most ostensibly neutral approach. The upshot of Eagleton's argument is that the social divisions of late eighteenth century, and particularly nineteenth-century England, found an imaginary re-unification in the integrated, holistic and harmonious idea of the aesthetic. So the arts are made to do (conservative) political work, precisely at the moment when they are held up as being above history and politics. Art and literature, as Matthew Arnold maintained, would step into the breach left by religion, but for Eagleton this means that they would operate as the ideological opiate that would keep the social hierarchy in place: 'the pill of middle-class ideology was to be sweetened by the sugar of literature' (26).

'Literature', it hardly needs to be said, is not the study of 'a stable, well-definable entity, as entomology is the study of insects'. As a discipline, Eagleton implies, English has operated as a Trojan horse for conservative and reactionary values, which ought to be decisively exposed and de-mystified. He carries many of the Foucauldian practices and beliefs of cultural studies – about the centrality of politics, the ubiquity of ideology, the contingency of value judgement – directly to the history of criticism as an institution. Since 'literature' is a dangerous illusion, the focus should shift on to the 'discursive practices' and rhetorical effects of *language* as whole. The polemical Conclusion to *Literary Theory: An Introduction* is a good-riddance obituary for the discipline of literary studies, a clarion call to move to cultural studies, to tear down the illusion that we can cordon off privileged manifestations of human creativity for special attention.

Eagleton has consistently insisted on the indelible politics of culture. His old enemy was the 'genteel amateurism' of the English dons and men-of-letters. More recently, however, in books like *The Illusions of Postmodernism* (1996) and *After Theory* (2003), he has upbraided the lack of interest that a great deal of postmodern theory has shown in political questions. Like an anguished Martin Luther, he now laments aspects of the movement he once heralded. He still respects the insights of Derrida, Barthes, Kristeva and others, but he bewails the excesses of the relativistic postmodernism that some of their disciples embrace:

> Cultural theory as we have it promises to grapple with some fundamental problems, but on the whole fails to deliver. It has been shamefaced about morality and metaphysics, embarrassed about love, biology, religion and revolution, largely silent about evil, reticent about death and suffering, dogmatic about essences, universals and foundations, and superficial about truth, objectivity and disinterestedness. This, on any estimate, is rather a large slice of human existence to fall down on. (*After Theory*, 101–2)

The problem is, though, that if you cosy up to radical systems of philosophy that purport to reduce 'truth' to language games and which relativize every aspect of human experience to the shifting arbitrariness of sign constructions and linguistic play, there is always the danger that your own political principles are going to fall under the same sceptical procedures. Antifoundationalist modes of thought will swipe the veil away from aesthetic value, revealing it in all its constructed, ideological shame. But can ethical and political values be sure that they too will not be exposed and critiqued? How does one ground concepts like responsibilities, human rights, or any other ethical 'ought' in this maelstrom? If you use a postmodern solvent to remove aesthetic ideology, how can you be sure it will not damage the ethical principles underneath?

In lamenting that cultural theory has thrown the ethical baby out with the aesthetical bathwater, Eagleton defends truth and morality against those postmodernists and relativists who see all truths as simply cultural constructions. If truth 'loses its force, then political radicals can stop talking as though it is unequivocally true that women are oppressed'. He does so in the name of political action – the same justification he used in his earlier work for replacing the idea of literature with that of 'discourse'. Unfortunately, it is dangerous to oust the sorts of value you dislike while keeping hold of those you do not. If beauty is relative, .then what makes virtue or morality different? Many people will agree with you if you say is it is wrong to oppress women, but proving that something is 'wrong' belongs to a different order of knowledge or truth from verifiable fact: it is a *value* judgement. If the question 'what is literature?' cannot be answered in the same way as an entomologist will tell you what an insect is, nor can the question 'what is right and wrong?'

IV

There has been much talk in the humanities about the 'end' of theory, some of it accompanied by sighs of relief or even whoops of joy, but more often asserted with an air of reflection and a palpable sense of 'where next?' Though the obituaries for theory have been written many times, often by those who wanted to bring on the death they described, it is not premature to recognize that theory wars are not the force they once were. It is not that the factions are simply shaking hands and compromising, still less are we returning to some pre-lapsarian Eden where the author is reinstated as king and happy schoolchildren are taught to recite by rote. It is rather that many of the precepts and debates of theory have been incorporated into wider academic practice. Theory no longer seems iconoclastic and youthful. Antagonism has ebbed and even those most associated with the theoretical movements of the previous generation have shown a propensity to reconsider long-established positions, to question the shibboleths that previously drove theoretical movements.

Not least of the re-imaginings is a new hospitality to the concept of the aesthetic. There are many signs – even amongst those closely associated with the razing of the old disciplines – that the aesthetic, the literary, and the question of artistic value are drawing increasing attention. Jonathan Culler, for instance, in his conclusion to the volume *What's Left of Theory?* (2000), calls for a regrounding of the 'literary' in theory, alleging that other agendas – race, sexuality, gender – have for the last 30 years skewed attention away from this properly central concern. Valentine Cunningham's *Reading After Theory* (2002) calls for a return to techniques of close-reading. The ideal relation of a reader to a text, he claims, is one of 'tact', a gentle and respectful attitude to the literary work that shows 'a rational, proper, moral even, respect for the primacy of text over all theorizing about text, a sensible recognition that though reading always comes after theory, theory is always the lesser partner in the hermeneutic game' (169). Thomas

Docherty, long at the forefront of theory in the UK, looks for a radical way of incorporating a new, renovated idea of aesthetic value, whose glorious uselessness will operate as a foil to the utilitarian, fact-dogged orientation of contemporary culture, including the continual administrative pressures to make education economical and vocational. ' "Business studies" ', Docherty suggests provocatively at one point, 'has no place in a university' (35).

As this remark suggests, this openness to aesthetics is not a renunciation of the political preoccupations of the past 30 years, but rather a development of it. The new interest in aesthetics is often intimate with the imagining of political possibilities at the level of form. The advocacy of interpretative tact, the renewed concern with the particular instance rather than the general rule, the allowance that texts might have a literary quality that is ineffable or inexhaustible – all have an implicitly political and progressive dimension. They seek to curtail *domination* of a text by the critic, to allow the text freedom in its own particularity. Approaching the work with some critical circumspection is, in this respect, a non-coercive, progressive way of reading.

The editors and contributors of *The New Aestheticism* (2003) argue that their consideration of the aesthetic is inseparable from social and political concerns. What theory tended to pillory and reject, they argue, was an outmoded view of the aesthetic. They insist on a dialectical view of the artwork which, while it recognizes the immersion of the artwork in a cultural location nevertheless maintains that the 'singularity of the work's "art-ness" ' which is not determined by surrounding political, historical or ideological questions'. The new aestheticism challenges what it regards as the anti-aesthetic consensus of so much cultural theory, but it makes this challenge not as a reactionary gesture but as part of a vanguard:

> One of the major limitations of the ideology critique of leftish criticism of the 1980s and 1990s is that in locating the aesthetic as a static or essentialist category or a dead "cultural weight", it then fails to take account for the enduring specificities of literature's cognitive significance. (5)

If structuralism and its heirs aimed for the general system, there has more recently been a reorientation towards the particular and the specific – looking anew at the individual artwork rather than considering it as part of a discursive framework.

This openness of theory to questions of aesthetics signals a new rapport between theories of criticism and questions of value. In the coming years, if this trend continues to develop, it will bear fruit in a pragmatic, focused criticism, where experts do not just theorize about particularity and specificity, but also evaluate the aesthetic dimension of particular and the specific literary works. There is then this opportunity for the renewed rapprochement between academic and non-academic criticism, a synergy which, as this book has sought to demonstrate, could richly benefit both parties.

There are, then, grounds for cautious optimism. Away from the theoretical coalface there are already signs of ententes between academe and journalism. Even as criticism has undergone radical dispersal and dilation in recent years, there is at the same time clusters of serious, evaluative criticism developing outside the universities. For instance, there are signs of renewed attention in the novel as a 'literary' form and as a vehicle for moral expression, a surge of interest in Henry James, for instance, and serious, sustained criticism on the novel by young authors like Zadie Smith (b. 1975). James Wood (b. 1965), an avowed evaluative critic of the novel, has built a career that has moved not from academia to journalism (the usual root) but rather from journalism to a university. He was chief literary reviewer for the *Guardian* and a senior editor for *The New Republic* and is now 'Professor of the Practice of Literary Criticism at Harvard', having held posts at other US higher educational institutions.

If the new aestheticism gains in its influence and delivers on its promises, it will not just valorise specificity and particularity in (paradoxically) general terms. It will produce criticism of specific and particular literary works. The 'practice of literary criticism' will not be a specially designated title but, once again, a common activity in university English departments. Another way in which 'Eng. Lit.' could profitably reconnect to its evaluative roots is to move closer to creative writing programmes. Creative writing has proved an irresistible draw as a university subject in recent decades, perhaps satisfying the appetite of literature lovers for the sorts of evaluative approach they are unlikely to obtain in a conventional English department. Unabashed as it necessarily is about evaluating literature, taught creative writing is an important arena for aesthetic judgement in a university setting. Such judgements generally happen ad hoc, or as a means to an end. Creative writing programmes rarely treat criticism as 'creative' (despite so recognizing other non-fiction genres, like biography and autobiography). But these programmes are nonetheless spaces in third-level institutions where literature is treated seriously as an end in itself, not just as an aperture to social or political context. If English were to move closer to creative writing, it would highlight affinities between creative and critical writing, as well as helping produce close connections between critics and artists. As movements like the Bloomsbury Group suggest, rapport between artist and critic can create energized contexts for artistic innovation and creativity.

Finally, if evaluative criticism is going to be admitted into university study, the discipline of English literary studies needs to make room for impressionistic, subjective response. More than all the subversive theoretical movements of the last 30 years, this would be a real challenge to the orthodoxy of the discipline. Ever since 'Eng. Lit.' sought to stiffen up the appreciative criticism of Quiller-Couch and Saintsbury with a good dose of practical rigour, the idea of responsive or impressionistic criticism has been regarded as a threat to the subject. But if creative writing and fine arts can be taught in universities then why not creative criticism? Critics, like creative writers, have a distinctive voice and outlook. Great figures in the history of criticism, like Hazlitt, Woolf or Empson, have a style as distinctive as a signature. Of course it will take years to master the art of criticism, but students should nevertheless be encouraged to embark on the process of finding their individual critical voice, rather than always mastering received procedures and theories. This is by no means to forsake standards or to turn the teaching of literature into simply the record of student enthusiasms. It does mean, though, that eloquence of writing, accuracy of expression, and the owning of language, should be part of an education in English literature. So should the idea that literature is worth studying in order to develop skills of discrimination and discernment. Academic rigour does not necessarily mean a scientific or empirical approach. Literary scholarship may be able to follow the objective, systematic procedures of history, but literary criticism comes closer to the creative arts. Of course critics should look for evidence to back up their claims. But there is bound to be a subjective element to evaluative criticism. In creative writing and fine art classes we tolerate the individually expressive. There needs to be space for it in university-taught critical writing too.

It is time to recognize that criticism is a craft and a literary form. It is the only mode of literary writing that you can be confident most people will have tried in their lives, since we all write critical essays at school. Yet it is perhaps the most dismissed and underrated literary form of all. The assumption that it is secondary and derivative devalues its currency. It is not deemed 'creative'. Yet who would swap one of Hazlitt's essays for a hundred bad poems or plays? Previously under-valued forms, like diaries and letters, have been elevated in recent years. But criticism is still regarded as a job for the eunuchs at the harem. Or at best a job, like the most basic DIY, that anyone can do with minimal effort.

Perhaps the critic is not dead, but simply sidelined and slumbering. The first step in reviving him or her is to bring the idea of artistic merit back to the heart of academic criticism. 'Judgement' is the first meaning of *kritos*. If criticism is to be valued, if it is to reach a wide public, it needs to be evaluative.

Works Cited

Amis, Martin, *The War Against Cliché: Essays and Reviews 1971–2000* (London: Jonathan Cape, 2001).

Aristotle, *The Poetics*, trans. Malcolm Heath (London: Penguin, 1996).

Arnold, Matthew, *Culture and Anarchy*, J. Dover Wilson, ed. (Cambridge: Cambridge University Press, 1932).

—, *Essays in Criticism*, Sister Thomas Marion Hoctor, ed. (Chicago and London: University of Chicago Press, 1968).

Barthes, Roland, 'The Death of the Author', in *Image Music Text*, Stephen Heath, ed. (London: Fontana, 1977), 142–8.

Beckett, Samuel, *Waiting for Godot* (London: Faber, 1965).

Brooks, Cleanth, *The Well-Wrought Urn: Studies in the Structure of Poetry* (New York, Harcourt Brace, 1947).

Carey, John, *What Good Are the Arts?* (London: Faber, 2005).

Culler, Jonathan, *Structuralist Poetics* (London: Routledge and Kegan Paul, 1975).

—, 'The Literary in Theory', in Judith Butler, John Guillory and Kendall Thomas, eds, *What's Left of Theory?* (New York: Routledge, 2000).

Cunningham, Valentine, *Reading After Theory* (Oxford: Blackwell 2001).

Docherty, Thomas, 'Aesthetic Education and the Demise of Experience', in John J. Joughlin and Simon Malpas, *The New Aestheticism* (Manchester: Manchester University Press, 2003), 23–35.

Dryden, John, *Essays*, W. P. Ker, ed., 2 vols (Oxford: Clarendon Press, 1900).

Eagleton, Terry, *Literary Theory: An Introduction* (Oxford: Blackwell, 1983).

—, *After Theory* (London: Allen Lane, 2003).

Eliot, T. S., *The Sacred Wood: Essays on Poetry and Criticism* (London: Faber, 1997).

Foucault, Michel, *Power/Knowledge: Selected Interviews and Other Writings 1972–1977*, Colin Gordon, ed. (Hertfordshire: Harvester Wheatsheaf, 1980).

Frye, Northrop, *Anatomy of Criticism* (Princeton, NJ, 1957).

Gross, John, *The Rise and Fall of the Man of Letters: English Literary Life since 1800* (London: Wiedenfeld and Nicolson, 1969).

Habermas, Jürgen, *The Structural Transformation of the Public Sphere: An Inquiry into the Category of Bourgeois Society*, trans. Thomas Burger (Cambridge: Polity Press, 1989).

Hare, David in conversation with Al Senter, *The Stage 125* (2005) (http://www.thestage.co.uk/stage125/profile.php/hare/).

Hazlitt, William, *Complete Works*, P. P. Howe, ed., 21 vols (London: J. M. Dent and Sons, 1930–4).

Hill, Susan, 'Just Who Do they Think They Are?' (13 November 2006), http://blog.susan-hill.com/blog/_archives/2006/11/13.

Joughin, John J. and Simon Malpas, eds, *The New Aestheticism* (Manchester and New York: Manchester University Press, 2003).

Kael, Pauline, *I Lost it at the Movies: Film Writings 1954–1965* (New York and London: Marion Boyars, 1994).

Kames, Lord (Henry Home), *Elements of Criticism*, 2 vols (Indianapolis, IN: Liberty Fund, 2005).

Kampf, Louis, 'Notes Towards a Radical Culture', in Priscilla Long, ed., *New Left: A Collection of Essays* (Boston: Porter Sargent, 1969), 420–34.

Kant, Immanuel, *The Critique of Judgement*, trans. James Creed Meredith (London: Oxford, 1952).

Keats, John, *Letters*, Hyder Edward Rollins, ed., 2 vols (Cambridge, MA: Harvard University Press, 1958).

Leavis, F. R., *English Literature in Our Time and the University* (London: Chatto and Windus, 1969).

—, *Nor Shall My Sword: Discourses on Pluralism, Compassion and Social Hope* (London: Chatto and Windus, 1972).

Pater, Walter, *The Renaissance: Studies in Art and Poetry*, Donald. L. Hill, ed. (Berkeley, CA: California University Press, 1980).

Perloff, Marjorie, 'What We Don't Talk About When We Talk About Poetry: Some Aporias of Literary Journalism', in Treglown and Bennett, eds, *Grub Street and the Ivory Tower*, 224–49.

Pope, Alexander, 'An Essay on Criticism', in *Poetical Works*, Herbert Davies, ed. (London: Oxford University Press, 1966), 62–85.

Ransom, John Crowe, *New Criticism* (Norfolk, CT: New Directions, 1941).

Richards, I. A., *Practical Criticism* (London: Routledge and Kegan Paul, 1929).

—, *Principles of Literary Criticism* (London: Routledge and Kegan Paul, 1924).

Rorty, Richard, *Achieving Our Country: Leftist Thought in Twentieth-Century America* (Cambridge, MA, and London: Harvard University Press, 1998).

Saldan, Raman, et al., *A Reader's Guide to Contemporary Literary Theory* (London: Prentice Hall, 1989).

Sidney, Philip, *The Defence of Poetry*, Jan Van Dorsten, ed. (London: Oxford University Press, 1966).

Sontag, Susan, *Against Interpretation and Other Essays* (London: Eyre Spottiswoode, 1967).

Treglown, Jeremy and Bridget Bennett, eds, *Grub Street and the Ivory Tower: Literary Journalism and Literary Scholarship from Fielding to the Internet* (Oxford: Clarendon Press, 1998).

Trilling, Lionel, *The Liberal Imagination* (New York: Viking Press, 1950).

Wilde, Oscar, *The Artist as Critic: Critical Writings of Oscar Wilde*, Richard Ellmann, ed. (London: W. H. Allen, 1970).

Williams, Williams, *Culture and Society: 1780–1950* (Harmondsworth: Penguin, 1963).

Woolf, Virginia, *A Room of One's Own and Three Guineas*, Morag Shiach, ed. (Oxford: Oxford University Press, 1992).

Additional Suggestions for Further Reading

Armstrong, Isabel, *The Radical Aesthetic* (Oxford: Blackwell, 2000).

Baldick, Chris, *The Social Mission of English Criticism, 1848–1932* (Oxford: Oxford University Press, 1983).

Barry, Peter, *Beginning Theory: An Introduction to Literary and Cultural Theory* (Manchester: Manchester University Press, 1995).

Bauerlein, Mark, *Literary Criticism: An Autopsy* (Philadelphia, PA: University of Pennsylvania Press, 1997).

Bennett, Andrew, and Nick Royle, *Introduction to Literature, Criticism, and Theory*, 3rd edn (Harlow: Pearson Education, 2004).

Bergonzi, Bernard, *Exploding English: Criticism, Theory, Culture* (Oxford: Oxford University Press, 1990).

Bernstein, J. M., *The Fate of Art: Aesthetic Alienation from Kant to Derrida* (Oxford: Polity Press, 1991).

Bowie, Andrew, *From Romanticism to Critical Theory: The Philosophy of German Literary Theory* (London: Routledge, 1997).

Brantlinger, Patrick, *Crusoe's Footprints: Cultural Studies in Britain and America* (London: Routledge, 1990).

The Cambridge History of Literary Criticism, 11 vols (Cambridge: Cambridge University Press, 1990)

Cassedy, Steven, *Flight from Eden: The Origins of Modern Criticism and Theory* (Berkeley, CA: University of California Press, 1990).

Collini, Stefan, *Absent Minds: Intellectuals in Britain* (Oxford: Oxford University Press, 2006)

Connor, Steven, *Theory and Cultural Value* (Oxford: Blackwell, 1992).

Court, Franklin E., *Institutionalizing English Literature: The Culture and Politics of Literary Study, 1750–1900* (Stanford, CA: Stanford University Press, 1992).

Culler, Jonathan, *Literary Theory: A Very Short Introduction* (Oxford: Oxford University Press, 1997).

Donoghue, Denis, *Ferocious Alphabets* (New York: Columbia University Press, 1984).

—, *The Pure Good of Theory* (Oxford: Blackwell, 1992).

Dworkin, Dennis, *Cultural Marxism in Post-War Britain: History, the New Left, and the Origins of Cultural Studies* (Durham, NC, and London: Duke University Press, 1997).

Eagleton, Terry, *The Function of Criticism: From the 'Spectator' to Post-Structuralism* (London: Verso, 1984).

—, *The Ideology of the Aesthetic* (Oxford: Blackwell, 1990).

The Edinburgh Encyclopedia of Modern Criticism and Theory, gen. ed. Julian Wolfreys (Edinburgh: Edinburgh University Press, 2002).

Eliot, T. S., *Selected Essays* (London: Faber, 1951).

—, *To Criticize the Critic and Other Writings* (London: Faber, 1965).

Fish, Stanley, *Professional Correctness: Literary Studies and Political Change* (Oxford: Clarendon Press, 1995).

Furedi, Frank, *Where Have All the Intellectuals Gone: Confronting 21ˢᵗ Century Philistinism* (London and New York: Continuum, 2004).

Goodheart, Eugene, *The Failure of Criticism* (Cambridge, MA: Harvard University Press, 1978).

Gould, Thomas, *The Ancient Quarrel Between Poetry and Philosophy* (Princeton, NJ: Princeton University Press, 1991).

Graff, Gerald, *Professing Literature: An Institutional History* (Chicago, IL: University of Chicago Press, 1987).

Guillory, John, *Cultural Capital: The Problem of Literary Canon Formation* (Chicago, IL: University of Chicago Press, 1993).

Hernstein Smith, Barbara, *Contingencies of Value: Alternative Perspectives for Critical Theory* (Cambridge, MA: Harvard University Press, 1988).

Leitch, Vincent B., *American Literary Criticism from the 1930s to the 1980s* (New York: Columbia University Press, 1988).

Lentricchia, Frank, *After the New Criticism* (Chicago: University of Chicago Press, 1980).

—, *Criticism and Social Change* (Chicago: University of Chicago Press, 1983).

McQuillan, Martin, et al. (eds), *Post-Theory: New Directions in Criticism* (Edinburgh: Edinburgh University Press, 1999).

Mulhern, Francis, *The Moment of 'Scrutiny'* (London: New Left Books, 1979).

Parrinder, Patrick, *Authors and Authority: English and American Criticism, 1750–1990* (London: Macmillan, 1991).

Said, Edward, *The World, the Text and the Critic* (Cambridge, MA: University of Harvard Press, 1983).

Scruton, Roger, *Modern Culture*, new edn (London and New York: Continuum, 2005).

Wellek, René, *A History of Modern Criticism, 1750–1950*, 8 vols (New Haven, CT: Yale University Press, 1955–92).

Williams, Raymond, *The Country and the City* (London: Chatto and Windus, 1973).

—, *Keywords* (London: Fontana, 1976).

Woolf, Virginia, *The Essays of Virginia Woolf*, 4 vols, Andrew MacnNeillie, ed. (London: The Hogarth Press, 1986–94).

Index

Printed in the USA
CPSIA information can be obtained
at www.ICGtesting.com
LVHW020839171024
794056LV00002B/295

9 780826 492807